Developing Training Courses

A Technical Writer's Guide to Instructional Design and Development

Developing Training Courses

A Technical Writer's Guide to Instructional Design and Development

Rives Hassell-Corbiell

Learning Edge Publishing
Tacoma, Washington

Published by Learning Edge Publishing, an imprint of The Learning Edge, P.O. Box 97041, Tacoma, Washington 98497-0041. USA
Telephone: (253) 588-5174. URL: http://www.lepublishing.com
Author's e-mail address: riveshc@lepublishing.com

Quantity discounts are available on bulk purchases of this book. Special editions or book excerpts can be created to fit specific needs. For information, please contact Learning Edge Publishing.

The following trademarks appear in this book: Access, DataBase Pro, FoxBase, Microsoft Word, Microsoft Project 98, and Myers-Briggs Type Indicator.

Although the author and publisher have made every effort to ensure the accuracy and completeness of the information contained in this book, we assume no liability for errors, inaccuracies, omissions, other inconsistencies, or use of the information contained herein. Any slights against people or organizations are unintentional. Readers should consult an attorney, qualified consultant, or other appropriate professional for specific applications of the content contained in this book to their training development projects.

Cover design: Robert Howard Graphic Design, Fort Collins, Colorado.

Library of Congress Cataloging-in-Publication
(Provided by Quality Books, Inc.)

Hassell-Corbiell, Rives.
    Developing training courses: a technical writer's guide to instructional design and development / Rives Hassell-Corbiell. – 1st ed.
    p. cm.
    Includes bibliographical references and index.
    LCCN: 00-193546
    ISBN 0970145403

    1.Instructional systems—Design—Handbooks, manuals, etc.
    2. Occupational training—Planning—Handbooks, manuals, etc.
    3. Technical writing. I. Title.

LB1028.38.H37 2001   331.25'92
        QB101-200012

Here's what people are saying about
Developing Training Courses

This is the only guide like it that I know of on the market. It has a logical format, clear instructions, and lots of practical examples. I think your *[Forecasting Training Tempests]* sections throughout are some of the best pearls of wisdom I've ever encountered. I really love the book. Highly recommended.

Peggy Jacobson, Ph.D., President
Technical Communication Consultants, Inc.
President, Puget Sound Chapter,
Society for Technical Communication
Seattle, Washington

This is the first book I recommend if you don't have time to make mistakes.

Clare Petrich, Owner, Petrich Marine Dock
Acting Executive Director, World Trade Center
Tacoma, Washington

This book provides an excellent starting point for technical writers interested in the field of technical training. [Rives has] created an important guide to this field that will be welcomed by many writers...[she has] the bases well covered.

Carol Perkins, Training Development Manager
Brooktrout Technology
Los Gatos, California

Finally! A foundation book for those of us so caught up in the technology of training delivery that we've overlooked the basics of how to develop good training. I've seen the author in action, and I know that this book is not just a theory. She has written this book from her own experience and success in developing good training.

Burkhard L. Berger, District Commodore
U.S. Coast Guard Auxiliary
Honolulu, Hawaii

Ms. Hassell-Corbiell uses her combination of talent, hard work, and years of experience to help technical writers enhance their knowledge base and increase their value in the workplace. Whether you are a novice or an experienced trainer, a one-person operation or a major corporation, if you need to pass knowledge to others through training, this is the book to buy. Study the information, view the examples, and use the templates to simplify the development process.

Pamela Coca, Technical Writer and Consultant
Owner, Write-On Communications
Member of Society for Technical Communication and
American Medical Writer's Association
Laguna Niguel, California

Acknowledgments

A project like this could not have happened without the tireless support of my husband, Clement. Thanks Sweetheart.

I owe special thanks to my peer reviewers, Peggy Jacobson and Carol Perkins, without whose comments I would be missing some important targets. Thanks also to my editor, Michael Lopez, who reminded me to say what I mean, to Dan Poynter, the owner of Para Publishing, who taught me how to organize this project, and Robert Howard, for the beautiful design of the book cover.

To bend obstacles to our purposes is a great step towards triumph.

—Victor Hugo, *Toilers of the Sea*

Table of Contents

Section 1:
Foundation

Skill Sets for the Future

Designing and developing a training course can seem daunting, but taken a step at a time, you can create effective training that makes a difference in the lives of your learners.

Training Development Is a Journey

A hiking experience I had a few years ago provides an apt metaphor for training development.

The rugged Na Pali hiking trail on the lush Hawaiian island of Kauai is steep, rutted, and rocky. It begins just *makai* (seaward) of a cave, and rises abruptly from a sandy beach. It is bordered by the navy blue Pacific Ocean on one side, and steep green cliffs covered with lush ferns on the other side.

The climb was difficult. Red dirt from the trail irritated my eyes. Roots and small waterfalls running across rocks on the trail were at the same time beautiful and treacherous. Rounding a kink in the trail, I was blasted with a thirty-knot wind. Clutching at my hat, I leaned against a rock to steady myself and rest. I peered down the cliff's edge at palm tree crowns, gauging how far I had climbed. Another hiker leaned his way up the trail and caught the same surprising blast I had, falling back two steps. I looked forward through half open wind-blasted eyes, and was struck by a view so stunning that it made my heart skip a beat—steep rounded cliffs fingered out into the water, stacked one behind another, into the horizon. I had seen photographs, but the beauty and scope far exceeded what had been captured on film. I lingered for a while, savoring the experience, then moved on.

Like that hiking experience, creating a training program can be a challenging uphill climb, with obstacles that can delay or stop you. But if you know your way and are prepared, you can enjoy what you experience during the journey.

There are rewards at the end of the trail as well—a sense of achievement, satisfaction when learners tell you what they will do differently as a result of your course, confidence to take on another challenge, a better leveraged skill set, maybe even a promotion.

Purpose of This Book

The purpose of this book is to guide you through the training development process. It focuses your attention on what is important, warns you about what can undermine your success, and provides a how-to strategy for reaching the summit of your project—course delivery—and returning to base camp—feedback, revision, and ongoing maintenance.

I believe that even if you are an experienced training developer, you will find that the suggestions, templates, resources, checklists, assessments, and samples included in this guide will remove rocks that can cause you to stumble. Real-life examples illustrate how to apply techniques. A section called "How to Forecast Training Tempests" is at the end of each development-step chapter and within selected chapter segments to warn you of process and organizational mudslides that can complicate your journey.

It is my personal goal that you enjoy the journey as much as the destination. I've drawn from 25 years of practical experience in the field as a performance consultant, instructional designer, developer, and trainer to make your trail easier to travel. This book is your guide for an interesting and safe journey—now and each time you undertake a training project.

Who Benefits

Training development can be costly and time-consuming. By knowing what questions to ask, what to do first, and what resources you need, you can develop a quality product within the budgetary and time constraints you have to work with. The ultimate beneficiary is the learner.

Technical writers, editors, project leaders, project managers, staff writers, and consultants will benefit from following this systematic approach to training development. Whatever your title, if your projects include writing documentation, policies and procedures, guidelines, tutorials, web content, and user help, you can learn how to redirect and build upon what you know to create effective training.

Cross-functional team members will also benefit from the concepts and practical applications in this book. They include intranet or extranet developers, multimedia developers, distance learning experts, web content editors, web designers, technical trainers, user interface designers, localization specialists, technical illustrators, and technical translators.

Use this guide to coordinate new or outsourced instructional designers, trainers, subject matter experts, and consultants with whom you will be working. Use it to ensure that terms, techniques, and processes will be uniformly applied across the project.

Who Are Technical Training Developers?

Who in the technical writing field develops training courses?

Informal surveys of STC members who attended my training development workshops over a period of one year revealed the following results:

- Prior to becoming technical communicators, they worked as engineers, software designers, administrative assistants, authors, factory workers, technicians, soldiers, accountants, teachers, nurses, and freight dispatchers, to name a few of the many professions represented.

- Corporate missions included product development, manufacturing, and services in areas and industries such as computer software, computer hardware, pharmaceuticals, credit card services, wireless communications, defense, aeronautics, transportation, energy, and airlines.

- They wrote in a variety of contexts, such as, software documentation, engineering policies and procedures, legal briefs, new hire guidelines, help systems, and global product marketing materials.

- Two-thirds of the learners in those classes had already completed, or were in the process of developing, a training course, which was remarkable, as I had expected first-time course developers who were anticipating the start of a project. They tried first to do it on their own, then realized what was involved, and sought resources to help problem-solve their project.

The implications of these findings are two-fold: that any technical writer can be assigned to develop a training course, irrespective of preparation or background knowledge; and that training development is not intuitive. It is a process that requires planning and a systematic approach.

The challenges that others have faced are included in this guide for you to benefit from. Their diverse experiences enrich these pages by pinpointing where the rocks and roots are likely to be in the path of your training development project. Anecdotes, real-life stories, and the solutions that were applied to their situations are here for you to learn from.

The Trend: Cross-Functional Skills

Training development is becoming an expected skill set for technical writers. The American Society of Training and Development (ASTD), a professional organization with over 70,000 members worldwide, reported, "In an information-based business economy . . . the race belongs to companies that build and harness their intellectual capital.*"

Place yourself on the leading edge of a business trend that will make you more marketable for years to come.

Over the past several years, I have noticed a trend in organizations and corporations for which I have worked, including governmental and a variety of other industries in several countries. During the interview process, when customers described the problems they wanted to solve, I realized that several were describing training needs. For each of those organizations, I proposed a training solution as part of the problem-solving package, and was hired over other consultants who had focused only on technical writing.

These organizations wanted a combined technical communication and behavior change solution, but did not recognize it until presented with the option.

Wondering how widespread this need was, I tested interest by submitting proposals related to training development to regional conferences of the Society of Technical Communicators. The proposals were accepted, seats for each session were filled, and people had to be turned away. There was definitely an interest among technical writers in training development. In fact, more than half had developed training. I offered longer workshops and they were filled. A community college recruited me to teach training development for their technical writing certificate program.

The trend is continuing, and now is the time to develop your training development skills. By applying the content within these pages, you place yourself on the leading edge of a business trend that will make you more marketable for years to come.

---

* Laurie J. Bassi and Mark E. Van Buren, "1998 ASTD State of the Industry Report," *T&D Journal* (January 1998).

Business needs are driving the marketplace to ongoing learning that is available 24x7 for employees anywhere in the world, and training-delivery technologies are becoming more cost effective, in the form of web-based learning.

Whatever learning methodology or technology is used, the training budget will be driven by competition. To retain the edge, employees need to keep up with the latest and greatest ideas, methods, and products. Training is the solution. The need for technical communicators to have cross-functional skills in instructional design and development is gaining momentum.

Corporate learners need venues that match their business needs. The marketplace is calling for on-demand training, available globally, either as a stand-alone event, or an adjunct to classroom training. Surveys conducted by the American Society for Training and Development (ASTD) indicate that:

- Technology training is the fastest growing segment of training budgets.

- CD-ROM or corporate intranet now delivers fifty percent of training interventions.

- Over 90 percent of training professionals are being required to justify the cost, benefits, and bottom-line impact of their training projects.

Technical writers who will be best prepared to meet the demand are the ones who expand their skill set to include training design and development. Technical writers need practical hands-on support in this cross-functional role, and this guide provides it.

Overview of Content

This book is divided into four sections. **Section One** provides a foundation for instructional design and development. Chapter 1 positions the trend toward training development as an expected skill for technical writers, and how *Developing Training Courses* addresses that trend. Chapter 2 directs you to hot topics with a quick start menu that points to answers you need today. Chapter 3 presents the training development competencies you need, and assesses which ones you have now. Chapter 4 forecasts stormy conditions that can undermine the success of a training project and tells you how to deal with them. Chapter 5 is an overview of what adult learners need, and describes how you can meet their needs.

Section Two is the core of the book. It describes each step of the systematic approach to training development that will make your training courses effective. It tells you what to do, how to do it, warns you of what can go wrong, and how to prevent or fix it. It includes examples, templates, assessments, and checklists for each

Technical writers who will be best prepared to meet the demand are the ones who expand their skill set to include training design and development.

step. Chapter 6 is an overview of systematic training development. Chapter 7 provides guidelines for planning a training project, and estimating the time it will take. Chapter 8 shows you how to collect information about your learners and what they need to know or be able to do. Chapter 9 describes the foundation-building strength of objectives and how to construct them. Chapter 10 shows you how to create tests that determine the level of learning. Chapter 11 shows you how to use a design document to ensure the success of the project, prepare for content development, and warns you of what can go wrong without one. Chapter 12 is an overview of content and materials development, which includes instructional techniques, methods, and technologies. Chapter 13 explains how to pilot the first-time delivery of the course, and verify the accuracy and appropriateness of content and design. Chapter 14 describes how to evaluate and revise course content. Chapter 15 includes tips for completing the course development journey.

Section Three describes how to manage training projects and customize existing material for use in your project. Chapter 16 helps you manage the instructional design process. It tells you how to prevent time and cost overruns, how to secure cross-department support, and tells you what parts of the project you can and cannot cut corners on. Chapter 17 shows you how to select and customize off-the-shelf courses. Chapter 18 provides guidelines for writing for international markets. Chapter 19 shows you how to repurpose documentation for training. Chapter 20 describes how to find, select, adapt, and use existing CGI, Perl, Java, and JavaScript scripts to automate training course activities.

Section Four is an active resource tool. The Appendices include a list of all of the job aids from the book conveniently located in one place, including templates, work sheets, checklists, and assessments. The Bibliography of References includes materials consulted for the content of this book. The Bibliography of Resources provides online, print, audio, and video references pertaining to each step of the training development process. It is organized into topics that include instructional technology, performance technology, e-learning, ready-to-use scripts, multimedia, international markets, and related topics of current interest. The Glossary includes training-related terms.

Quick Start

What is Quick Start?

Quick Start answers questions that most first-time training developers have. It is designed to point you to answers you need to have now. Quick Start is not intended to teach you how to develop training courses—reading each chapter will do that for you. Quick Start allows you to focus in on a small fire, and extinguish it quickly.

How to Use Quick Start

Find the topic under which your question fits, and scan for the questions that training course developers most often ask.

Training Process

- **How is training development different from technical communication?** See Table 3.1 in Chapter 3, *Assess Your Training Development Skills.*

- What do I need to know about adult learning and why? See *Adult Learners*, Chapter 5.

- **What are the steps in developing training?** See Chapter 6, *Overview of Systematic Training Development.*

- **How do I know I'm doing the right things?** Follow the eight-step systematic approach—follow the procedures and guidelines in Chapters 7-14.

- **How do I organize the flow of topics in the course?** Use the learner and task analysis results as initial guidelines. See Chapter 8, *Analysis.* Then make a final determination based on the learning objectives. See Chapter 9, *Objectives.*

- How can I transform existing documentation into training materials? See Chapter 19, *Repurposing Documentation to Training.*

- **How do I know that the training I'm developing will work?** If you have defined the problem, determined that training is the solution, developed a sound course goal, performed a learner analysis and task analysis, based your learning objectives on analysis results, developed tests that reflect what the learners need to know, developed interactive content using real-life situations, and revised your course based on evaluations from your learners, your course cannot help but achieve its goals. Use the eight-step process in overviewed in Chapter 6, and detailed in Chapters 7-14.

- What are the most common mistakes that first-time training developers make?

  - Skipping analysis—it is time consuming, but provides the basis and validation for objectives, tests, course design, and course content.

- Providing too little support for the instructor in terms of materials, directions for exercises, and answers to tests or questions. See the section on instructor materials, Chapter 12, *Content Development*.

- Not clearly defining the problem, or determining whether training is the solution. For guidelines, see "Is Training the Solution?", Chapter 4, *Forecasting Stormy Conditions*.

- Not establishing clear and frequent communication with stakeholders and subject matter experts. See Chapter 7, *Project Plan*, for questions to ask your stakeholders.

- **What training techniques are most effective?** Read about instructional methods and media in Chapter 12, *Content Development*.

- **How can I tell when trouble is developing?** See the end of each training development chapter, Chapters 7-14, and read the symptoms that forecast training tempests.

Cost of Training Development

- **How do I estimate cost for my project?** Use the guidelines for what to include in the project plan, Chapter 7.

Politics and Team Members

- How can I get subject matter experts and other sources to give me the answers I need? See "Politics," Chapter 8, *Analysis*.

- **How do I navigate touchy political matters regarding the training project?** See "Politics and Winning Tactics," Chapter 4, *Forecasting Stormy Conditions*.

Time Estimating and Customizing

- **Can I customize training we already have? How do I select commercially available training?** There is an entire chapter dedicated to those topics. See Chapter 17, *Customizing Off-the-Shelf Courses*.

- **How can I estimate how long training development will take?** See Chapter 7, *Project Plan*, and refer to the tables with guidelines for estimating the time each step of the course development process will take.

Your Comments Are Welcome

Is there a question you think should be included in Quick Start? Please let me hear from you. Send comments to: riveshc@lepublishing.com

Assess Your Training
Development Skills

Introduction to Competencies

A competency is an ability to make decisions or perform actions that are critical to the successful performance of a job. Training developers demonstrate specialized competencies. There is an overlap of some competencies between training developers and technical communicators. That means that technical communicators bring abilities they can use to develop training. However, there are important competencies they need to add to their repertoire.

This chapter provides an overview of the competencies that technical writers bring to the training development table and describes additional skills that technical writers need in order to develop training.

Competencies of Effective Technical Writers

Technical writers are part of a family of professionals called technical communicators. According to the Society of Technical Communicators (STC), whose membership exceeds 25,000, major job categories include technical writers, editors, graphic designers, multimedia artists, web and intranet page information designers, translators and others whose work involves making technical information understandable and useable.

What competencies do technical writers have? Expected core competencies, based on a list of competencies developed by Illinois State University and STC[*] include:

- Planning

- Coordination

- Research

- Information organization

- Copy writing

- Illustration planning

- Project review

- Document production

- Proficiency in language composition

- Technical expertise or aptitude

These competencies support the results of a 1998 survey[**] of STC members, which revealed that fifty percent of respondents had an educational background in English, journalism, or communication.

---

[*] Peggy Jacobson, Ph.D., "So You Think You Want to Be a Technical Writer?" STC Job Fair presentation, Bellevue, Washington, 8 November 2000.

[**]Interpreted from data in "1998 Survey of STC Consultants and Independent Contractors Special Interest Group (CICSIG)," Society for Technical Communication, online, 17 July 2000, unavailable.

These disciplines develop competencies that rely on structure, format, vocabulary, and organization.

Thirty percent of respondents in the same study had an educational background in science or engineering. These technical areas of study focus on methodical, logical, and measurable approaches to situations that involve things, functions, and systems. This background develops competencies in systematic approaches to solving problems, using proven techniques, and developing or following practical guidelines.

All of these competencies are important for technical writers, and all of them contribute to effective training development. However, there are important competencies and skills that are required in addition, which include:

- Skills for interacting with, leading, or motivating people to behave in a different way.

- Competencies related to interpersonal skills, relating people to things, relating people to each other, or creating systems that change behavior.

Competencies of Effective Training Developers

ASTD publishes job descriptions of training and development professionals. The description for training developers states that employers prefer educational backgrounds like education, educational psychology, human resources management, instructional technology, and communication.[*]

> "Learning is not a spectator sport."
> —D. Blocher

The focus of these disciplines is on people, behaviors, human interactions, and the dynamics of change. A competency that these disciplines develop is how to interact with people, how to shape behavior, and understanding that people cannot be predictably and

---

[*] "Instructional Designer," American Society of Training and Development, *ASTD Trainer's Toolkit: Job Descriptions in Workplace Learning and Performance* (Washington, D.C.: ASTD, n.d.), 66.

uniformly changed. They learn about motivation, influence, value systems, persuasion, and negotiation.

How Do Training Outputs Differ?

A superficial comparison between documentation and training indicates key differences between their products.

Documentation	Training
• Is an information product	• Enables through experiences
• Increases understanding	• Develops skills and knowledge
• Focuses on a task: how to get from A to Z	• Focuses on job performance: learning what to do and how to do it
• Is organized for information retrieval	
• Scope: one task broken into steps	• Is organized for behavior change
• Customers are called users	• Scope: collection of skills and knowledge required to perform a job
	• Customers are called learners

Table 3-1. Key Differences between Documentation and Training Products

Technical writers help users solve problems by making technical communications understandable and useable. Training developers help learners develop skills and knowledge competencies that they will apply by thinking and acting differently on the job.

What Competencies Are You Starting With?

Structuring tasks with the intention of creating behavior change is not something that technical writers do every day.

Structured learning includes:

- Creating a learning goal that addresses a problem

- Developing performance objectives that support the learning goal

- Determining learner needs

- Selecting training methodologies that support performance objectives

- Developing tests that assess learning

- Evaluating how learning outcomes align with the learning goal

Each of the preceding activities is a step in building a training course. These are not activities routinely performed for documentation.

The following table is a checklist for assessing what training developer skills you have. You might have several already. By the end of Section Two, you should be able to check off every item.

Bridging the Gap

You can bridge the gap between technical writing skills and training development competencies by:

- **Following a systematic approach to training design.** This will ensure that you remember to do the important things in the right order, and with the most productive effort.

- **Using proven techniques.** Do what has worked for training professionals.

- **Using practical templates.** Implement guides, forms, checklists, and other tools that will make the training development process easier for you and more effective for the learners.

Competency Self-Assessment		
Training Developer	**Current Skill**	**Notes**
Can apply a screening process to determine whether projects are appropriate for training development		
Can implement a systematic approach to creating training courses that includes:		
Developing a project plan		
Conducting a needs assessment		
Performing all forms of required analysis		
Writing and appropriately sequencing performance objectives		
Developing performance measurements		
Developing a design document		
Appropriately selecting and applying instructional methods and strategies		
Developing instructional materials		
Evaluating training material, instructional delivery, and learner feedback		
Can anticipate most unproductive training project situations		
Can coordinate efforts with team members, subject matter experts, and project stakeholders		

Table 3-2. Self-Assessment of Existing Training Developer Competencies[*]

---

[*] The self-assessment was based on a list of competencies published in William J. Rothwell and Henry J. Sredl, *ASTD Reference Guide to Professional Human Resource Development Roles and Competencies*, 2nd ed. (Washington, D.C.: ASTD, n.d.).

Sage Advice

Live as if you were to die tomorrow. Learn as if you were to live forever.

—Gandhi

The real voyage of discovery consists not in seeking new lands, but in seeing with new eyes.

—Marcel Proust

Education is what survives when what has been learned has been forgotten.

—B. F. Skinner

Forecasting
Stormy Conditions

This chapter addresses three large-scale issues that can forecast conditions that endanger or undermine the success of a training project. When you see conditions that herald a storm, you can prepare yourself by donning waterproof clothing, carrying an umbrella, and finding shelter. In a similar way, if you recognize conditions that can damage your project and know what action to take, you can protect the integrity and success of your project.

Stormy conditions that apply to all phases of a training project are presented in this chapter. Conditions specific to each step of the training development are presented at the end of each chapter in Section Two, and, in the case of analysis, at the end of sections for each type of analysis. By the end of Section Two, you will be able to recognize stormy conditions related to training development, and learn what you can do to ride out the storm and stay dry.

to recognize stormy conditions related to training development, and learn what you can do to ride out the storm and stay dry.

Writing is Writing, Right?

There are differences in technique, focus, and preparation between technical writing and training development. Anyone who assumes that all writing makes use of the same sets of skills invites disappointment. Assuming that writers can develop effective training, because training includes writing, is a condition that can bring on stormy weather, and dampen the success of the project.

Technical writers know that the same techniques will not work uniformly well with all assignments. Doing so can cause problems. A help project for business users differs from software documentation for systems engineers. An instruction sheet differs from a marketing brochure. Technical writers know that differences involve more than visual format of the finished product. Differences include content, tone, style, approach, vocabulary, scope, and depth, to name a few.

Training courses have special characteristics. Training differs from technical writing in a fundamental way. Where technical writing focuses on the communication of written (or multimedia) content, training focuses on a learning experience. An effective learning experience creates behavior change. Consequently, the training developer must:

- Identify what the learners know and are able to do.

- Identify what the learners must be able to do, by when, and to what level of proficiency.

- Bridge the gap between where learners are now to where they need to be.

Shelter from this storm is provided by the eight-step strategy for instructional design in Section Two.

Is Training the Solution?

A stormy condition can be forecast if two questions are not answered from the outset:

- What is the problem that must be solved?

- Is training the solution to this problem?

Training can be an important professional development tool. Unfortunately, professional development might be relegated to low priority when training is used as a foil for another agenda, such as:

- A bandage for an organizational wound, which redirects attention from the problem area and defers required large-scale change.

- A stepping-stone for a stakeholder's personal visibility or promotion.

- A leading edge marketing strategy, which promotes an advanced technology or an initiative at the expense of an effective learning experience.

- A sweeping one-size-fits-all solution to a complex problem.

The people whose agendas are satisfied by a training course can deem it successful, but successful training is not the same as effective training. Effective training identifies and meets the needs of the learners.

You can offset the brewing of this storm by asking the following questions during the initial discussion about the training project assignment:

- **What is the problem that the training is supposed to solve?** How is the problem related to a business need such as, time, cost, customers, image, strategy, or competition? For example, the problem is that new hire customer service employees are unable to answer irate customers courteously.

- **Will training solve the problem and how?** If you hear an answer that does not include professional development of the learning population, the question has not been answered. Appropriate answer: We want them to have a collection of words and phrases they can use that will defuse an angry situation. Inappropriate answer: We want to fix the problem. The latter does not realistically address the issue.

- **Is training the only solution?** The best solution? Part of the solution? Listen carefully, and consider alternatives to and combinations with training, such as follow-up activities, at-the-job coaching, ongoing feedback, and problem-solving advice from supervisors. If there were required job procedures to follow, would job aids be useful? Would a mentoring process help reinforce training? Should the training be alternated with time on the job, then a more advanced level of training?

If the answers you get indicate that training is required, then the eight-step development process will help you define the problem and the solution.

Politics and Winning Tactics

Inclement conditions can be precipitated by a belief that training and technical writing are subordinate activities. In large corporations, training has traditionally been a cost center. That means that internal training costs the company money, and that training organizations have not been held accountable for a return on investment. Talented subject matter experts, such as technical, field, or sales personnel, are often rotated into or borrowed for temporary training assignments, but with the understanding that they will be rotated out before they can become *stale* or *out of touch* with leading edge innovations. There is a saying, which some people believe, that says *those who can—do, those who can't—teach.* As a consequence of this kind of backward thinking, requests from training team members might not receive first priority. Additionally, that kind of thinking is a detriment in a knowledge-based organization. Your tact, political savvy, and ability to put a strategic value on your project are valuable business skills for getting cooperation from the best SMEs, getting funding and resource needs met, and getting project stakeholders to understand, back, and present your project's best interests to those they answer to.

Tact, political savvy, and ability to put a strategic value on your project are valuable business skills.

Never Say It Can't Be Done

A stormy condition can develop whenever someone hears the word *no*. Instead of saying a project cannot be done, suggest alternatives that can keep the sun shining over your customer and you. Consider the following example.

Let's say that that an internal customer asks for a scripted instructor guide—a guide that includes narrative for everything the instructor should say and do—and a student workbook to support a five-day course that is not like any pre-existing course. They expect to recruit trainers from employees, who are neither subject matter experts nor trainers. The customer has scheduled the first delivery date four weeks from today and wants to know when you can get started on development.

Let's say you have already read this book, and quickly calculate what will be required to perform this task. You conclude that the customer wants forty hours of face-to-face training delivery, which, to meet his demands, requires one page of material for every minute of teaching time, excluding graphics; that if you had a staff four times the size of the one you have to work with, they would have to work 80 hours per week; and that with the team you have now, the delivery date is 32 weeks short. What should you do?

A. Say you are having surgery that requires long-term recuperation, and sincerely regret that you're going to miss this opportunity.

B. Ask if he is insane, and refuse the project.

C. Agree to his terms, plan to work day and night until the due date, and anticipate that you will need a month of sick leave at the end of the project.

D. Nod your head and say, "That sounds like an interesting project. Let's discuss your expectations and what I need from you to get that job done."

That Sounds Like an Interesting Project

The answer is D: "That sounds like an interesting project." The first step in scattering a potential storm like this one is to establish rapport. Invite the customer to negotiate by offering some form of encouragement and indicate that you are listening. Become a collaborator. If you stick to the role of subordinate, or appear uncooperative, this can become an interaction about power, rather than about getting a job done well. Position yourself as cooperative, flexible, open to ideas, reasonable, capable, and dependable. If you establish rapport, you can share in managing the process with your customer.

Pre-Assignment Project Management. Your objective in the pre-project phase is to demonstrate interest, ask questions that shape the project, secure your stakeholders as active sponsors, and, where necessary, negotiate terms that will target a more realistic outcome than the one being proposed.

Demonstrate interest. You want to reinforce the idea that you are a team player. A training assignment is not something that you can take and run with by yourself. My experience has been that people's careers are often tied to their proposal of and the success of a training project. The person who presents the project to you or to your project leader is likely the one who will be most hurt by a failed project or elevated by a successful project. Your corporate success will be linked to theirs. This is important to understand. Your challenge will be to focus on the needs of the learners, while juggling the interests of stakeholders.

Shape the project. Shape the project by finding out what your customer's requirements and constraints are, providing a reality check, renegotiating the terms, and securing them as an ally.

- Ask your customer to tell you more about the learners, the challenges, and the constraints they face—time, money, and resources. Ask why the project is important to them personally.

- Who are the learners? What do they do, where are they located, how many are there, how long have they been with the company, what will they know coming in, what prerequisites (training or job performance) must they complete, how does this course fit into their curriculum? Will they be trained at their home sites or travel to one location? Is this a one-time, over time, or ongoing project? Will learners consider this training punishment, reward, preparation, or orientation? What do the learners need to know or be able to do by the end of the course?

- Why do they need the course in two months rather than some other time? Why is the due date not negotiable?

- Who or what is driving this project? What will the success of this project do for them?

Be proactive, not reactive. Express informed opinions. Offer your recommendations.

- Provide a reality check. Say something like "Based on what you have requested, this is what (time, money, and effort) will be required."

- Show them the math—how much development time is required and how that is or is not compatible with their deadline.

- Tell them what you *can* do. Suggest ways to meet their objectives. For example, the delivery date for the preceding example has an unrealistically short time line.

- Suggest alternatives. The time line can possibly be met if the customer agrees that a scripted instructor guide is not needed for the first training delivery. A solution might be to provide instruction using a team of subject matter experts who can provide prepared slide presentations that relate to the course objective. The student guide can be compiled from their presentation slides, and organized into chapters with title pages and a course road map. Later development can use these presentations for core content material.

- Negotiate terms. Tell your customer what you will need from them. For example, if getting the job done on time will require more resources, ask for those resources. Specify what you need and when you need them. Consider what you will need for each step of the development process. Make no final commitments until you have created a design document. There is no way you can get a handle on what the training assignment will require until you do some preliminary research. You don't want to lock yourself into a situation that will restrict your ability to meet the deadline.

Secure stakeholders as active sponsors. Reinforce their commitment and support, and set their expectations. You have promised that if they give you x, y, and z, you will deliver a quality course on time and within budget. If the stakeholders give you what you say you need to get the job done right and on time, you could be legitimately held accountable if you miss your delivery commitments, but they could also suffer in terms of prestige, opportunity, political standing, and the like. They want you to succeed. They have a vested self-interest in your success.

Continually update and communicate with the customer. For the project in the preceding example, the delivery deadline was presented as firm, so if you discover that you underestimated money or manpower requirements to meet the deadline, inform the customer right away. The development team, which might only be you, comprises the only players moving forward on the project. The customer can only watch and wait. The customer depends on you to make the right moves. You run the plays, but they can lose (or gain). Keep them in the communication loop with updates and status checks every day or two. Set their expectations as you go. Allow no surprises.

Adult Learners

What Adult Learning Is

Adult learning is the study of how adults approach learning experiences, what their priorities are, what motivates them to learn, and what techniques work best for them.

Many books, articles, and web sites are dedicated to the topic of adult learning theory. Many of them are cited in the bibliography of this book. I encourage anyone who earnestly wants to study the topic to begin with authors Robert Mager and Malcolm Knowles.

The purpose of this chapter is to identify what adult learners want and what a training developer needs to do to stimulate adult learning. I have distilled what has proved to be important to adult learners in my experience.

What Adult Learners Want

What motivates adult learners to learn? Studies reveal a number of factors, but they can be summarized into two major motivators: to satisfy their interest, or to be rewarded.

* **Interest.** The learner who is motivated by interest wants to know more because the topic is stimulating, provides an escape, or satisfies curiosity.

* **Reward.** The learner who is motivated by reward realizes that knowing about or being able to do a thing can lead to something he wants to have, be, or attain, such as a promotion, being better liked, keeping a job, becoming richer, stronger, sexier, or smarter.

What Can You Do to Stimulate Learning?

Adult learners do not want to feel embarrassed, demeaned, insulted, devalued, or stupid. Sometimes that message can be sent inadvertently by jumping into an unfamiliar topic without bridging to it with something familiar, or starting at a level too advanced for your learners.

A training developer stimulates learning by offering what learners are hungry for and in bite-size pieces that they can get their minds around.

You will discover what is on your learners' mental menus by following a systematic approach to course development that includes assessing needs, finding out about the learners and their work environment, carefully designing the course goal and learning objectives, developing course content and materials that support and reinforce the objectives, and revising content based on evaluations and criteria test results.

Stimulate learning by including the following strategies in your training course:

* **Know your learners.** Adult learners might challenge you to prove what the training will do for them. You need to understand why they need this training, what it will do for them, and what the consequences of not having it are.

- **Answer questions that are important to them.** Adult learners are impatient with course content that does not address issues that are important to them or to the performance of their jobs. Course content should answer questions they most often ask or, if they do not know what questions to ask, it should include answers to questions they need to know answers for.

- **Address situations that limit their success.** Situations that cause people to feel stuck in one place need to be recognized, not ignored or glossed over. If a car tire is stuck in mud, you do not continue to spin the tire in place—doing so digs a deeper hole. You put a piece of cardboard or sand underneath to provide traction—a different surface from which to gain traction. Sometimes people need traction to get mentally unstuck.

- **Show them how to overcome barriers.** That means that you need to know what barriers they face, what solutions have worked for others, and how they can make the solutions work for them.

- **Build on what they know.** If the topics and issues are foreign to them, how will they be able to apply the content to their lives? They cannot learn if they cannot make connections. Develop content in such a way as to lead them from what is familiar to what is unfamiliar through examples, analogies, and structured learning experiences.

- **Solve real problems.** Provide examples that solve problems that they most often face or are most likely to face. Make the content realistic and believable.

- **Give them time to share experiences with one another.** Networking with peers to solve problems is an informal learning strategy that many adult learners expect to exercise. If an opportunity to do so is not built into the course, learners will do so informally over breaks or after class. If there is no venue for benchmarking their experiences with others, the need might surface on the course evaluation forms.

- **Omit topics unrelated to what they need to know.** Make content relevant to their jobs, region, and work practices. Training courses are not like education courses. Education courses include theories, concepts, and material that do not directly relate to real-world applications. Training courses should directly relate to real-world applications.

Example: How to Increase the Value of a Learning Experience

Imagine that several friends ask you, the neighborhood green thumb, to teach them how to create flower gardens in their back yards. With this goal in mind you jot down a list of topics that you think are important and interesting.

Tentative Topics	
• Challenges and rewards of growing roses • Costs • Flower seeds and bulbs • My visit to tulip farms in Holland • Shape and size of garden	• Soil • Tools • When the flower club next meets • Where to shop for materials

Table 5-1. Initial List of Topics

After you complete your list of tentative topics, you phone each of the neighbors to set a time and date for their class. The first neighbor mentions that he is looking forward to smelling and enjoying a variety of healthy colorful flowers when he returns each Friday from his out of town business trips.

The second neighbor you phone mentions how different the sandy soil in her yard is from the clay she grew up around.

The last neighbor you phone says how much he is looking forward to learning about how to protect his future flowers from pests but still attract butterflies.

During that conversation, your learners revealed what was important to them. You amend your notes to include the following topics.

Final Topics		
Relevant		**Not Relevant**

• Flowers
  – Shape
  – Fragrance
  – Color
  – Height
  – Light
    requirements
  – Water
    requirements
  – Attractive to
    bees, birds,
    and butterflies
  – Care of
• Cost
• Effort to
  maintain
• Fertilizers
	• How long to
	  build
	• Materials
	• Mulching
	• Planning
	• Resources
	• Shape and size
	  of garden
	• Soil features
	• Soil preparation
	• Tools needed
	• Treating pests
	• Watering
	  systems
		• Biology of
		  trees
		• History of
		  roses
		• How plants
		  are grown
		  in a hot
		  house
		• My visit to
		  tulip farms
		  in Holland
		• When the
		  flower club
		  next meets

Table 5-2. Final List of Topics

Adult learners value learning that is interesting and rewarding. You can create interesting and rewarding training courses by following a systematic process. How to do this is the topic of Section Two.

Section 2:

What to do and How

Overview of Systematic Training Development

Training is often developed in a pressure-cooker environment. Urgent deadlines seem to correlate with product rollouts, new policy, strategic or marketing initiatives, company growth, and a change in politics.

The rush to react to each of these situations can smother the success of your project unless you are guided by a systematic approach to training development.

The following chapters detail each of eight progressive steps to building an effective training course. I embrace this eight-step model because it is comprehensive, adaptable, and easy to use.

Training Development Models

There are many commercial and academic training development models that describe the instructional design and development process. It can seem complicated. I have seen models that have from four to twelve steps. They are represented by circular, round, square, and linear flowcharts. From my point of view, they all include the same tasks, packaged differently to reflect a learning theory or to provide a brand association.

A Rose is a Rose

You might hear the training development process referred to by several names. The most commonly used are: training development (TD), instructional design and development (IDD), instructional development (ID), instructional systems design (ISD), and ADDIE. ADDIE is an acronym for a development model that includes: analysis, design, development, implementation, and evaluation.

A training professional can describe specific differences between systems design and course development, and compare the focus among several instructional design or adult education models. If you have that level of interest, you can direct your search to the fields of instructional technology, instructional design and development, or adult education.

A Systematic Approach

A systematic approach is important to ensure that the organization, structure, and instructional integrity of your course are sound. The eight-step training development model you will be introduced to in the next eight chapters is based on proven behavior change techniques. It is performance-based. It does not align to one learning theory, but comprises the best of cognitive, behavioral, and adult learning theories.

Each of the next eight chapters defines the step; describes its outcome, how it builds on the step preceding it, how it prepares you for the step that follows it, how to perform the step; and provides how-to instructions, guidelines, and examples.

Systematic Training Development
1. Develop a project plan
2. Perform learner, task, and training environment analyses
3. Develop learning and performance objectives
4. Design a testing strategy and develop test items
5. Develop the course design
6. Develop course content
7. Pilot the course, verify content and design
8. Evaluate learning, revise content

Table 6-1. This Eight-Step Systematic Approach to Training Development Will Ensure That You Create the Best Training Course You Can

The steps build on one another—one step provides the foundation for the next step.

Usability

Your target audience might include learners who need modifications that accommodate to hearing, sight, or movement limitations. Ask questions during each course development step that will alert you to those needs, such as:

- Are there members of the target audience who require special equipment or services? If so, budget for additional development and delivery costs, to include time, facilities, and specialized content.

- Are there computer-use adaptations we need to consider? If so, budget for, requisition, and include those adaptations during the course design and content development steps.

- Will multilingual sign language professionals be required? Other professional aides?

Let's get started.

Step 1—Project Plan

A project plan should precede any course development. It is the first step of the training development project.

What It Is

Project planning is the foundation of an effective training program. Planning directs your efforts and resources toward a proposed outcome. The deliverable document resulting from this step is a written project plan that will be submitted for approval to project stakeholders. Once it is approved, the plan will be used by project team members to guide their initial course development tasks.

A project plan is a decision tool. It enables the planners to focus and direct the development process, and to justify the expense of time, money, and effort that they project will be required to create the training course.

Levels of Project Plans

There are three levels of project plans.

Corporate training project plans describe the strategic impact of training initiatives within the corporation. For example, a rapidly growing high tech company, for which I helped revise a number of internal sales and systems engineer training courses, made a commitment to provide ongoing professional development opportunities and product education available to all employees, anywhere in the world, 24 hours a day. This was a strategic reaction to fast international growth in a quickly changing environment.

Curriculum project plans include a collection of courses that have a common goal, and oftentimes the order in which they should be taken. A management development curriculum plan that I helped develop at AT&T several years ago included twenty-two instructor-led courses to be completed over a period of two years. The curriculum was divided into several tracks that coincided with the manager's specialty, such as operations or human resources. The plan included time lines, a selection process, attendance requirements, and a syllabus for each course—although a bare bone curriculum plan can include little more than working course titles, descriptions, prerequisites, and the order in which the courses should be taken.

A curriculum plan can include instructor-led as well as alternative avenues to learning, such as at-the-job training, college courses, or conference attendance. Alternatives should be considered where classroom training is not available, not cost effective, or inappropriate. For example, apprenticeship programs for power utilities require hands-on experience. Many colleges and commercial training organizations offer courses that might meet the needs of your learner.

Courses in a curriculum project plan can seem unrelated, but must focus on the desired outcome of the curriculum. If, for example, the outcome is to prepare new hire help-desk personnel to correctly diagnose and fix phoned-in customer problems, the curriculum could include technical product knowledge, customer service skills, documentation research skills, and telephone system use.

The curriculum project plan should be cohesive and targeted. It unifies training efforts for a learning track.

Course project plans detail one course. In a large corporation, it might be included in a curriculum project plan or a corporate training project plan. If it is, then you will have a ready place to start your planning. It is easier to revise an existing plan than to develop one.

Each training course project should be launched with a project plan. Project plans provide direction and focus. Of the three types of project plans, this is the type of project plan you will most likely develop.

Components of a Course Project Plan

The project plan has two key purposes: to direct and focus your training development efforts, and to help make decisions about the training project. A project plan can alert you to potential problems and design constraints. For example, planning forces you to think about what you are going to do and what resources you will need to do it. If your deadline were six weeks away, then you would not decide to develop a 40-hour interactive online course, which requires from 100 to 400 hours of development time per hour of delivery time.

The course project plan should incorporate the following elements:

1. Tentative course title

2. Definition of the project scope

3. Identification of the target audience

4. Identification of key course topics and generic course activities

5. Estimation of development time

6. Required resources

7. Course duration

8. Outline of the course development budget

Your project plan is only as good as the questions you ask when developing the plan. Each component of the project plan is detailed below, with examples and guidelines for developing it.

1. Develop Tentative Course Title

The course should have a name that reflects its purpose. Save catchy phrasing for chapter or sub-titles in the final material. Although not glamorous, a title like *Selling Internetworking Solutions for Enterprise Account Managers* can catch the attention of a busy account manager, and help him make a decision to attend the course based on the title alone. A title like *Knock 'Em Dead Sales Skills* is a great title, but offers no clue about the focus of the course. Is it for beginning, intermediate, or advanced sales people? Is it for account managers who sell solutions, or for retail sales clerks who sell washing machines?

2. Define Project Scope

The scope of the project should be defined in terms of general content boundaries. For example, the scope of a sales training course might be to introduce product features and the business needs for which they are a solution, or to enable telephone installers to splice fiber-optic cable in simulated workplace conditions. The scope can also detail what will not be covered in the course. For example, the sales course mentioned above, that introduces product features, might not include sales techniques or products that are currently sold, but that are at the end of their life cycle.

A clear course goal should be included in this section of the project plan. The course goal is a one-sentence description of what the course is intended to accomplish. It is closely aligned with the scope of the course, and is expressed in terms of the intended outcome for the learner.

If the scope is:	Course goal could be:
To introduce product features to account managers, including the business needs for which the products are solutions	To enable account managers to present product solutions that address customer business needs
To teach telephone installers how to splice fiber-optic cable with a high degree of accuracy, and in any weather conditions they might face on the job	To enable telephone installers to splice fiber-optic cable

Table 7-1. Examples of Transforming Scope Descriptions into Course Goals

The course goal does not usually include conditions, such as *with 95% accuracy*, or *under realistic work conditions*. Conditions are used where certification, graded evaluation, or some measurable performance level are required.

Conditions are a component of course objectives, rather than of a course goal. Objectives define and support the course goal. They comprise the third step of the training development process and will be detailed in a later chapter.

Scope	Example Questions	Sample Answers for Help-Desk Course
	Why is training needed?	To improve our customer service rating for technical assistance
	What should the course goal be?	To teach help-desk personnel customer service skills
	What should the course include, not include?	It should include people skills; it should not include technical content
	When the learners finish this training, what should they be able to do?	Deal with angry customers, answer questions professionally
	Under what circumstances?	Simulated work conditions
	To what level of competency?	They need to be able to describe options and demonstrate some proficiency
	With what burden of proof?	A certificate of completion, and maybe pass a test

Table 7-2. Questions that Help Define Scope

3. Identify the Target Audience

The target audience is whom the training is for. The plan should include their current level of knowledge and skill, the anticipated or documented gaps in their knowledge and skill, knowledge and skills they need to acquire, how many people need to receive instruction, and what special considerations they might require in terms of shifts, hours, culture, language, and geographic location.

How can information about the target audience shape your training project? Assume that your initial questions about your target audience reveal that they are enterprise account managers. They sell expensive computer internetworking hardware to very large corporations. Each account manager has a sales quota of over one million dollars a year. They are located in six regional offices in four states and two Canadian provinces. Any Canadian version of your training product is required by Canadian law to be in French and English. Account managers are not expected to travel to receive training, or to attend classes on Saturday or Sunday.

This information provides clues about how long the course can last, what day of the week it can begin and end, and that translation costs might be part of the budget. The large sales quota and enterprise designation tell you that the accounts include very large corporations, costly products, complex product solutions for the end customer, and a long sales cycle.

Your training course will need to reflect the nature of the target audience's workplace experience while also providing examples that are realistic for them.

The following table includes examples of questions to ask when you are developing the target audience component of the project plan.

Target Audience	Example Questions	Sample Answers for Power Lineman Course
	Who is the course for?	Journeymen power linemen—men and women
	How long have they been with the company?	Seasoned employees with from 10 to 25 years of service
	What do they know about the topic already?	Some have hot stick experience
	Do all of them need the training or just some?	Only those who will be hot sticking
	How will you determine who needs it?	Those assigned to Pierce County dam projects
	How many people need to be trained? Locations?	About 45 in four field offices and HQ
	Will training be compulsory or voluntary?	Compulsory, to be monitored by supervisors
	What travel, time, or budget constraints does the training design need to consider?	There are some union contract restrictions—a combined total of 12 working and training hours per day
	What prerequisites do they need?	Journeyman lineman ticket, pole-top rescue
	In what settings will they use what they learn in this course?	On a pole or in a bucket with energized lines

Table 7-3. Questions that Help Define Target Audience

4. Name Key Course Components

Critical topics and activities that should be included in the course are called key components. For example, critical topics for a consultative selling course for enterprise accounts might include:

- How enterprise customers make decisions

- Strategies for accessing large accounts

- How to recognize customer needs

- How to evaluate options

- Knowing the competition

- Resolving customer concerns

- Negotiations and concessions

- Implementing account maintenance strategies[*]

You might wonder how you can know what topics are appropriate. After all, you might be unfamiliar with the target audience, the content, or both. Your only resources at this point are the stakeholders and your personal knowledge.

If I am unfamiliar with a topic, I find it helpful to bullet a few generic items. For example, if the project is a how-to course on counting migrating salmon, critical topics could include an overview of why salmon are counted, where to find migrating salmon, the procedure for counting them, what tools and equipment are required and how to use them, and reporting methods. Remember that the critical topics in the project plan are proposed topics. In the next step, which is analysis, you will collect hard evidence about your target audience and what they need.

Critical activities are instructional methods that should be included in the course. For example, instructor-led lecture, case studies based on true stories from the field, and sales team role-plays. The

---

[*] Example topics for consultative selling were taken from Neil Rackham, *Major Account Sales Strategy* (New York: McGraw-Hill, 1989).

activities should reflect the goal of the course. If the goal is to introduce salmon-counting techniques, then lecture, reading, and videotapes might correlate with that goal. If the goal is to develop salmon-counting skills, then hands-on simulations that use counting equipment and live fish might be appropriate.

Key Components	**Example Questions**	**Sample Answers for Web Developer Course**
	What are the most important things for the learner to know about this topic?	Network layers, major types of software, types of software development languages, how a web site works, how to read URLs, and how to troubleshoot web-related network problems, roles and responsibilities of web development team members, customer roles.
	What should they be able to do?	Demonstrate proficiency with web page design tools, network management software, and network security software. They should be able to diagram web-related network architectures and map fairly complex web sites.

Table 7-4. Questions that Help Define Key Course Content Components

Questions about key components should reveal a wish list of topics. The analysis phase of the training development process will determine which topics are critical, nice to know, or missing from the list.

Ask for as much clarification as you can get. Be sure that terms like *fairly complex web site* are clearly defined by the time you complete the analysis step. Clearly defined means worded in behavioral (testable) terms. *Diagram a fairly complex web site* could become *diagram a six-level web site having thirty pages and include navigation links from each page.*

5. Estimate Development Time

Time seems to be the greatest adversary of a training developer. There never seems to be enough of it. Design decisions in a project plan are based on one of two time alternatives: a non-negotiable delivery date, or an estimated delivery date. A non-negotiable delivery date drives design decisions. An estimated delivery date is derived from decisions made about the course design.

When the project has a non-negotiable delivery date, use the following time estimate guidelines to partition the designated time, and set boundaries on the time you can spend on each development step.

A rule of thumb for quick estimates is to allow 30-40 hours of development time per hour of training delivery for an instructor-led course. This estimate includes all eight development steps.

Here are guidelines for more thoughtful estimates for each step of the training development project:

Development Time Estimates	
Project planning. One to four days.	The time this step requires depends on how clearly the project idea has been developed, whether resources have been discussed and committed, and whether a project timeline has been determined.
Analysis. This step requires 20-25 percent of project time.	Analysis includes learner analysis, task analysis, training environment analysis, and the analysis report.
Learner analysis. Two to five days for each day of training.	Highly technical or complex tasks require more time. Diverse and geographically dispersed training populations will require additional time. Add travel days to your time estimates.
Task analysis. Four to six days per day of training.	Time in this analysis depends to a great extent on how accessible the people and experts are with whom you are working, and how quickly they respond to material that you submit to them for review and comments. Add time to task analysis when task performers are learning new or unproven tasks—these take more time due to ongoing revisions of the task, as task performers learn how to do the task, or as they explore ways of improving how to perform a new task.

Table 7-5. Time Estimates for Each Training Development Step

Development Time Estimates, continued

Training environment analysis. One to four days.	Since this analysis often creates questions about resource availability, which take time to answer, allow for four days for this analysis. If it takes less time, you have stored bonus days, and if not, you will not find yourself behind schedule early in the project.
Analysis report. One to four days.	Include time spent in meetings that discuss the results of your analysis. Add a half-day for every three days of training over five.
Course objectives. One day for each training day.	
Criterion test items. Two days for each training day.	
Course design. Four to six days per day of training.	The output of this step is the design document. The final selection of instructional methods and media should fit the needs of the learner and the non-negotiable constraints of the project.
Content development. This step requires 25 to 40 percent of the project time. Estimate 15 to 25 days per day of training.	This step could take more time if you must develop multimedia and computer-based material, which include scripting, casting, editing, and production. Estimate 15 to 25 days per day of training, which includes developing, formatting, editing, and proofing student materials, instructor materials, exercises, activities, and supporting materials. Add time for audio, visual, and multimedia content development.

Table 7-5, continued. Time Estimates for Each Training Development Step

Development Time Estimates, continued	
Content development., continued	Content development depends on instructional methods, media, supporting materials, and activities. For example: instructor-led classroom training requires about 20 hours of content development per hour of training delivery.
Interactive media. 200-400 hours per training delivery hour	Interactive multimedia instruction can take between 200-400 hours to develop per training delivery hour. *CBT Solutions* magazine (August/September 1995) reported that the average for an experienced developer is 220 hours.
Video production. Up to eight weeks for a simple video	If you are outsourcing, get an estimate from the vendor—expect production to take up to eight weeks. Some tasks require the participation of a project team member. Whether you use a vendor or produce the video in-house, budget the time for a team member to be involved in developing the script and monitoring filming. Even if you outsource the script, someone from your team needs to meet and liaison with the outsourced writer. Have a team member present during filming to ensure that appropriate content, focus, and tone are captured.

Table 7-5, continued. Time Estimates for Each Training Development Step

Development Time Estimates, continued	
Content development., continued Audio production. Budget 10 to 20 hours per hour of audio output.	As with video production, a training development team member needs to at least collaborate or liaison regarding script content and editing decisions, and to be present during taping.
Pilot and verify. Two days per day of training.	
Ongoing revision. Allow four hours per hour of training.	Allow four hours per hour of training for minor edits and updates. Extensive changes are equivalent to content development and should be estimated using development time guidelines.

Table 7-5, continued. Time Estimates for Each Training Development Step

6. Identify Required Resources

The project plan should anticipate human and capital resources that are required for all phases of the project, including design, development, delivery, and maintenance. This includes identifying project team members, subject matter experts (SMEs), equipment, facilities, and services. Services can include leased lines, intranet connections, servers, satellite connections, airport or hotel shuttle service, meals, and printing.

Carefully think about each phase of the project, and anticipate all personnel, hardware, and services costs that you can. Your sources might include the accounting department, the facilities manager, the information technology group, and other managers who have developed project plans.

Resources	Example Questions	Sample Answers for Software Overview Course
	What facilities will be required for training delivery?	Company-owned training rooms in five U.S. cities, and rented facilities across Canada.
	What equipment will be required and will it be available on needed dates?	Will need computer terminals for every two participants, and connections to the company intranet. Dates and class size are yet to be determined.
	What hardware, software, or equipment will be required by the instructional development team?	Access to the software and its documentation for each team member, hardware that exceeds minimum software requirements, and access to the company intranet.
	What roles need to be filled on the project team, and who will fill them?	One project manager (RHC), who will double as editor, a web page designer (KSC), and two course developers (BHL and CSC).
	What SMEs will be required, in what areas of specialty, for how many hours per week, and what leverage do you have to ensure timely cooperation?	Need access to two SMEs experienced in the application of this software, and one expert user for 10 hours per week for 6 weeks.

Table 7-6. Questions that Help Identify Required Resources

7. Determine Course Duration

Duration refers to how often and for how long the course is expected to be delivered, for example, a four-day course to be delivered once a month for one year. The duration of the course can influence cost and resource decisions, as well as design and content development decisions. It can indicate a need for follow-up expenses, such as course maintenance.

A course that will be delivered once in a small local office would not receive the same revision and maintenance considerations that an ongoing training course for a rapidly growing company would receive.

Duration	Example Questions	Sample Answers for Newly Hired System Engineers Course
	How many times will this course be delivered?	Once each month
	Over what period of time?	At least 18 months
	How long does the course need to be?	Five days, or about 40 classroom hours
	Is the content expected to change?	Products will be introduced and retired during the training delivery period
	What is a reasonable time frame for updates, corrections, and revisions?	New products should be inserted prior to each monthly delivery, corrections and minor revisions quarterly

Table 7-7. Questions that Help Define Course Duration

Answering questions about duration will help you decide what instructional design and instructional methods to choose, how instructors will be selected and prepared, and whether you need to plan for course maintenance, including updates, revisions, and corrections.

8. Outline the Budget

The budget includes anticipated expenses, such as salaries of the course development team and subject matter experts, travel related to course development, travel related to course attendance, equipment purchase or lease, facilities rental, web site design, online operations, and printing.

Consider what you might need to outsource. Outsourcing should be considered when the cost of doing it yourself, which includes learning, equipment, software, and reworking, is higher than an estimated cost from an expert.

You will need to clarify the scope of the budget. Will it include only the expenses related to the development, pilot, and revision of the course? Will it include the cost of equipment and facilities that need to be acquired for course delivery? This cost needs to include how many days the course will last and the number of times the course will be held. Will the scope of the budget include total costs to the company? This cost needs to include the travel expenses of all participants, and possibly their salaries.

You also need to know what constraints you have for outlining the budget. Will you be designating how an already allocated amount of money will be spent? Are there restrictions on how the money can be spent? Will the budget you outline be used to request funding?

Budget	Example Questions	Sample Answers for Product Sales Course
	Has an amount been set for the cost of this project?	$150,000
	Is more funding available if needed?	Not for development. Maintenance is a separate line item and can added to the amount above.
	What is the process for obtaining funding? Who do we go to? What steps or forms are required? Who must review the request? Who signs off?	This project is a collaboration between corporate training and marketing. See Joan in accounting for details.
	What activities does the budget for this project include?	All costs related to course development, except software purchase and equipment leasing costs. It includes travel related to course design and development. It does not include course maintenance. It does not include costs for equipment, services, or facilities rental for course delivery.

Table 7-8. Questions to Ask Before Detailing the Budget

Have you been told you have carte blanche? It would be wise not to take this literally. I have yet to meet a manager who funded budget requests without question. This offer usually means that when you submit your budget, the people holding the purse strings will consider any reasonable request. If they see any item in the budget that appears to be fluff, they will question it. If you cannot defend the value of what you include, the budget for those items will not likely be provided. Your project plan needs to support the value of anything important enough to budget for.

It makes sense to research budgeting last because there is so much crossover information that pertains to it collected for scope, target audience, key components, resources, and duration.

Tools and Templates to Use

The project plan is a report. You can create it in any word processor. You can use planning tools such as Project Manager, and spreadsheet programs such as Excel to create time lines and task breakdowns for the project plan, but they are not required.

Word processors that can create tables and line drawings are sufficient. The review function in word processors like Word enable you easily respond to suggested changes from multiple reviewers.

A Gantt chart or PERT chart can help you visualize the project timeline, flow of tasks, and placement of resources.

The length of a project plan can be five pages or fifty. It is determined by the amount of detail you have available and the complexity of your project.

The format of a project plan might be determined for you. If it is not, decide whether to use narrative, bullets, information mapping, or whatever style will make your plan easy to read and understand. Consider the format that your stakeholders expect, have the time for, or are most comfortable reading.

This Step Is Complete When

The project plan is complete and you are ready to move into analysis when:

- All stakeholders have signed off on the project plan.

- An account has been set up against which project expenses can be billed.

- All development team members can clearly describe the project and their descriptions are almost the same.

How to Forecast Training Tempests

Stormy training development weather, which can include bottlenecks or delays, is forecast by any of the symptoms below:

- Resistance to committing requested resources

- Postponement of funding for the project

- Disagreement about whom and to what level of time the subject matter experts will be committed

- Expectation that team members or SMEs will complete the project in addition to the normal duties of their everyday jobs

- A transient delivery date

Step 2—Analysis

A training project plan provides focus, determines a course goal, sets boundaries around the course, and forecasts what resources are needed to get the job done.

Analysis is the second step of the training development process. It is the investigation and research phase of the project. The overall purpose of analysis is to identify what skills and knowledge the learners require to perform that part of their job that satisfies the course goal. Collecting information about the learner, the tasks that comprise the job, and the environment in which training will occur accomplishes this.

Overview

In the context of training development, analysis means determining what the training population does now, what they should be able to do after training according to the course goal in the project plan, and what knowledge and skills they need to close the gap.

Analysis can also identify bottlenecks, errors, decision points, tools, interactions, and performance discrepancies between what should be done and what is done. The data collected in analysis will be used to:

- Provide factual grounding for course content.

- Indicate what kind of design infrastructure will best support the content

- Reveal gaps, omissions, or errors in the project plan.

- Uncover prerequisite knowledge and skills.

- Prepare the training developer for the next training development phase of creating performance objectives for the course.

The analysis step includes collecting, interpreting, and applying data.

- Data collection includes interviewing, examining documents, and observing people working.

- Interpreting data includes organizing, ranking, prioritizing, finding patterns and assigning meanings to the data collected.

- Applying data includes developing connections between what the analyses tell you and the appropriate methodologies for course design, content, and delivery.

What to Do

Analysis can be done in many ways, but to create effective training, there are three types of analysis that cannot be neglected:

- Learner analysis

- Task analysis

- Training environment analysis

Each is detailed in this chapter.

How to Determine Sample Size

If you have a training population of 100 or more people, plan to interview 15% of them. If the training group is 25 or less, interview all of them.

Guideline for Determining Sample Size	
Size of Training Population	**Sample Size**
100 or more	15%
75	25%
50	50%
25 or less	100%

Table 8-1. Guideline for Determining How Many People to Sample During the Analysis Step

Who to Sample

Your sample should include a mix of:

Competent performers. These are experienced people, who do the job as it should be done.

Master performers. These are outstanding job incumbents who have found innovative, cost-saving, or timesaving ways to do the job as it should be done, or do the job in a way that exceeds expectations.

Other people can tell you about the target training population:

Supervisors and managers. They can provide guidelines for what should be happening on the job, what is missing, and what they suspect the problems are. They are a step removed from the performance of the job, and are observers. They can provide a comprehensive view of how job performance affects the department, organization, or company.

Subject matter experts. Also called SMEs, they have content expertise. They can tell you what the learners most often come to them for and can suggest effective ways that job incumbents and SMEs can work better together.

If your target population is geographically dispersed, be sure to interview a percentage of the target training population in each region. There could be regional or cultural differences in procedure, priorities, and challenges. You can reduce cost and time expenditures by conducting some interviews via telephone or Internet.

By omitting culturally or geographically diverse groups from the analysis step, the resulting course can:

- Overlook key challenges or barriers

- Omit important examples

- Include inappropriate material or offensive activities

- Include out-of-date material

- Lack credibility

- Conflict with local, legal or work practice requirements

Dealing with Barriers

You might encounter a manager or supervisor who challenges your need to contact an important source of information. On several occasions, I have been informed that I did not need to speak with SMEs or anyone from the target population—that the manager could tell me anything I needed to know. My recommendation is to document this exchange, copy every stakeholder involved in the success of the project, and be able to support your requirement to conduct a sound learner analysis. Absence of the right data at this step can undermine the effectiveness of following steps, and consequently, the effectiveness of the course.

How Much Time to Spend on Analysis

Analysis is a time-intensive step that, if done well, can save time in each of the following steps. I like to budget 20 percent of the project time for this step.

Rushing the project is a phenomenon that a training developer can experience at any point in the project, but often during analysis and content development—the two most time-consuming steps. There always seems to be someone asking how far along you are, and why you are not further along. This is normal. Stakeholders are looking for tangible evidence that their project is moving along, and at this point the only tangible evidence they have is a project plan. You can prepare for this eventuality by clearly understanding why you need to perform each step of the instructional design and development process. You can reassure interested parties by being able to describe what you have accomplished, what you are doing now, what step is next, and how you will apply what you are doing now to the next step.

An informal part of the project is updating stakeholders about the project. They usually want to know if it is on time, and if there are bottlenecks or barriers.

The following sections of this chapter define each type of analysis, describe how to perform them, describe what can go wrong, and how to get back on the trail.

Learner Analysis

Learner analysis collects data about what the learner should be able to do in order to be effective on the job. This requires interviewing both master performers, people who are already doing the job well, and the target training population, a cross-section of people who will attend training. The outcome of this analysis is to detail learner attitudes and aptitudes.

Attitude is a state of mind or feeling. Learners' attitudes can indicate trends that a training course needs to be aware of. A training developer should examine attitudes about the job, the tasks that must be learned, and barriers or obstacles that are perceived by the learner.

Ignoring the power of attitudes can cost people their jobs. A situation like this happened early in my career, and perfectly illustrates the need for learner analysis when designing training.

I was employed by a telecommunications manufacturing company, which planned to implement a computer-based accounting system in its plants nationwide. At this time, all accounting was done by hand, using mechanical adding machines. My assignment was to develop a two-day, computer-based training course that would teach them how to use the computer-based accounting system. I did not question that the length of the course and the delivery method had been decided before planning or analysis. It was an exciting opportunity to use leading edge technology to create one of the first computer-based courses.

My project partner and I interviewed 165 accounting clerks in seven plant locations around the country. Three people that I interviewed were particularly memorable because of the high visibility their situation created, and the trend they represented.

Three accounting clerks worked at the same plant in the Northeast. Two had been with the company for over 25 years. One had been with the company for less than two years.

Both long-timers expressed fear about using a computer-based system—one because she feared that it would reduce her to the same expertise level as an entry-level clerk, and the other because she was afraid of permanently erasing important data. The third clerk was an entry-level clerk who was eager to learn about computers.

Within six months after completing the course, the entry-level clerk was a supervisor; the one who feared she would erase important data was pleased to find that her work was faster and easier; and the one who dreaded loss of her prestige had retired.

These three people reflected what we found to be a trend in each of the seven regions—that there were three distinct groups of people in our training population:

- The early adapters, ready to jump onboard the new technology, who train with nothing to lose and everything to gain

- The fearful but willing adapters, who would lose (prestige, efficiency, comfort) in the short term but believed they would be better prepared to grow with the company

- The fearful and unwilling adapters, who were willing to be left behind at the station because they believed there was no way to make up for what they would lose

This experience is memorable because if the training development process had been done correctly—if the instructional method of the course had been preceded by, and chosen based on, analysis, objectives, and instructional design, then more people might have retained their jobs. Objectives could have been developed to address the three different needs and kinds of adapters. Training delivery methods that did not escalate the threat of failure, for example, could have been chosen. An instructor-led course, which is traditional (comfortable, familiar, includes an interactive human to human component), could have retained some of the fearful but unwilling adapters. Instead, a highly visible leading edge technology drove the project, which in turn drove out some long-time employees, who feared not only failing the learning process, but being unable to apply the new technologies to their jobs.

Aptitudes are innate abilities that are required or preferred. Aptitudes include a way of thinking or an ability that comes easily, comfortably, and naturally. Aptitudes for a job are qualities that make the job easier, more enjoyable, and more interesting for the person doing it. For example, a software designer who finds solving math problems fun and challenging, and who has the patience to work things out, is more likely to code more fluently, figure out errors more easily, and persevere until all of the errors are found and fixed—and have fun doing it.

Every profession has what it calls *naturals*—the people who are among the best in the profession, and who seem to have achieved that distinction based largely on natural ability. The natural swimmer glides smoothly through the water with a relaxed and powerful stroke. Aptitudes might include broad shoulders, powerful arms, a long reach, the ability remain relaxed under stressful conditions, and a large oxygen exchange capacity. Aptitudes for a natural parent might include a nurturing presence, patience, and being attentive.

How would you define aptitudes for a natural sales person—someone who makes you want to give them your money and thank them for taking it? Would aptitudes include friendliness and trustworthiness? Or would an important aptitude be the ability to be perceived as friendly and trustworthy? Identifying aptitudes can be tricky.

Aptitude is not a selection criterion that you are likely to find formally defined. In a work climate where opportunity must be extended equally to all, aptitude is less likely to be a criterion because measuring it is difficult, and assessing it is likely to be subjective.

If aptitude is so hard to identify and quantify, then why would you look for it? How would you recognize it? Having identified it, how would you use it?

Try to document how master performers approach their jobs, make decisions, and interact with others.

Master performers, the people who are best at their jobs, have qualities that might be teachable. If you can identify what made the job easy or difficult to learn, what techniques master performers use that others do not, or suggestions they have for entry-level performers, then the overall performance of everyone could be improved.

Information about aptitudes can be collected from supervisors or job incumbents.

Aptitudes provide an important clue about how a job can be done more effectively. My suggestion is to probe for aptitudes. Find out what master performers think newer performers should know. Try to document how master performers approach their jobs, make decisions, and interact with others.

When you do content analysis, job descriptions can provide clues to preferred aptitudes, such as "must like dogs" or "must be comfortable with repetition." Generally, aptitudes are not included in job descriptions as such. After all, how can an employer legally prove the presence or absence of an aptitude? How can an employer turn down a competent, qualified person based on an unmeasured and undocumented aptitude? A useable aptitude would have to be quantifiable and measurable—testable.

Competencies are what learners already know how to do. They are abilities that the learner brings to the job and that support doing the job. Examples include an applicant for a clerking job who is able to add a list of three-digit figures without a calculator, an applicant for a technical writing job who has four years of experience using Word software, or a customer service representative applicant who demonstrates interpersonal skills.

When you conduct a learner analysis, you need to determine what the required competencies are for the job, whether they must be present at the start of the training course, and if so, at what level of expertise.

If you do not determine pre-course competencies, then you might not understand what is wrong when the bulk of your learners fail to achieve course objectives.

The cost of overlooking basic competencies is demonstrated by a widespread situation that large corporations face today. For many years, employers assumed that high school graduates could read, write, and do math at a twelfth grade level. They hired high school graduates who could do their jobs adequately, but with difficulty or errors caused by their low level of reading, writing, and math skills. Companies currently spend millions of dollars in remedial programs for employees. Today, an entire industry has developed around teaching basic reading, writing, and math skills to adults.

Knowledge and skills that you want to investigate are those that are specific to on the job requirements. They include the use of tools. Tools include software, equipment, foreign language proficiency, keyboarding, large equipment operation licenses, safety certifications, and any other knowledge or skill required for effective performance on the job.

The job-related knowledge and skills you identify during learner, content, and task analysis will comprise most of the training content.

Sources for Data Collection

A learner analysis can be performed by:

- Conducting face-to-face, online, or telephone interviews with managers, subject matter experts, master performers, competent performers, and customers

- Observing at-the-job performance

- Reviewing documents related to job performance

Answers to Look For

By the end of the learner analysis, you want to have the following answers about the learners:

- What do they need to know and be able to do?

- What would be nice for them to know or be able to do, and why?

- What situations do they most often face?

- What questions do they most often ask?

- In what areas do they most often fail or underachieve? Why?

- What subjects and issues are important to them, the company, and to the customer?

- What makes a difference in the way they perform on the job?

- What really happens compared to what should happen?

- Will training alone solve the problem(s)?

- What bottlenecks or barriers prevent them from performing well on the job?

The answers you receive might require that you ask additional questions to delve deeper, or that you alter direction to pursue an issue.

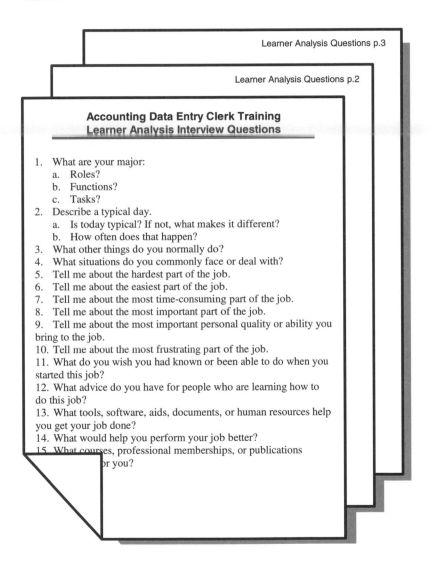

Learner Analysis Questions p.3

Learner Analysis Questions p.2

Accounting Data Entry Clerk Training
Learner Analysis Interview Questions

1. What are your major:
   a. Roles?
   b. Functions?
   c. Tasks?
2. Describe a typical day.
   a. Is today typical? If not, what makes it different?
   b. How often does that happen?
3. What other things do you normally do?
4. What situations do you commonly face or deal with?
5. Tell me about the hardest part of the job.
6. Tell me about the easiest part of the job.
7. Tell me about the most time-consuming part of the job.
8. Tell me about the most important part of the job.
9. Tell me about the most important personal quality or ability you bring to the job.
10. Tell me about the most frustrating part of the job.
11. What do you wish you had known or been able to do when you started this job?
12. What advice do you have for people who are learning how to do this job?
13. What tools, software, aids, documents, or human resources help you get your job done?
14. What would help you perform your job better?
15. What courses, professional memberships, or publications
    or you?

Table 8-2. Example of Learner Analysis Interview Questions

Setting up Interviews

Preparing for your interviews with the contact organizations can streamline your time and effort.

* Establish a relationship with the organization whose people you need to interview. Establish one contact person who can reserve a meeting room, schedule interviews, let you into the building, and troubleshoot for you during the day(s) that you conduct interviews.

* Draft a letter to come from you or the host company to the employees and their bosses that includes what you will be doing, why, and what you want from them.

* Set ground rules with management at the host location about anonymity, and what information will be shared with them.

* Agree on a number of interviews and method of selecting interviewees.

* Estimate how long each interview will take—estimate long rather than short. It is more acceptable to return people to their jobs early than late.

How to Interview

The purpose of each interview is to get as much relevant information as you can. One goal you should have is to make the person you are interviewing comfortable and to establish your trustworthiness with them. You can set the mood with the following checklist of items.

Interview Introduction Checklist	
✓ **What to Do**	**What to Say**
At the start of each interview, introduce yourself and the company or organization that you represent.	Hello, my name is Holly Smith. I'm a training developer from an outside company called The Learning Edge.
Explain the reason for the interviews.	Treeland Logging has hired me to develop training for new plant equipment engineers.
Explain why the employee was chosen to be interviewed in a reassuring way	I've been told that you know this job inside and out *or* that you have received recognition for the job you are doing *or* that you have been doing this job for a long time—and can tell me everything I need to know
Explain the general boundaries of the interview	I'd like to ask questions about what you do on the job and what you think will help others do the job well.
State how much of their time you need.	I'd like about 15 *or* 30 *or* 60 minutes of your time—that's what most of the interviews have taken.
Set ground rules for the interview process	Anything you say stays in this room. Please feel free to ask me questions about the training project.

Table 8-3. Guidelines for Beginning an Interview

Although the time for each interview has already been planned for and arranged with the employer, it is a matter of courtesy to the employee to state how much of their time you need. If you need more time, stop, state that you have reached the agreed time limit, and ask if they have more time that they can spend with you. Make sure you give yourself enough time when you extend the interview. Once can be indulged, but twice can be annoying.

If after two or three interviews you find that you need more time, inform your contacts, so that they can adjust the expectations of the people involved.

If you have to interview several hundred people, consider facilitating a group interview. Be sure to also set aside time to conduct individual interviews: what people reveal in front of others can be different from what they will reveal privately.

Set ground rules for the interview process that assure the employee's anonymity, demonstrate respect for them, and explain your behavior. For example:

- *Anything you say stays in this room.*

- *Your name will not be put with the notes. I'll take notes about what you say, but I keep the record of who I interview separate from what they say.*

- *If management asks for feedback from me, it will be in the form of a summary, not a copy of the notes I take.*

- *I'll ask you questions. I'm not looking for a right answer. I'm looking for information that will help others learn to do what you do. Please answer in the best way you can.*

- *I may ask questions that seem picky or detailed. I am not challenging what you say, but am trying to clarify my understanding. I'm trying to find out what you do, how you make decisions, and how you know what to do next.*

- *Please feel free to ask me questions.*

Interview Dilemmas and How to Deal with Them

Employees can be apprehensive about job-related interviews. You are asking them to tell a stranger about how they do their jobs. They cannot be certain where the information will go, or how it will be used. They have only your word.

Situations that could compromise your credibility come in packages that could surprise you. Over the space of twenty-five years, several situations have jeopardized my trustworthiness, and undermined the success of data gathering. Sometimes, I did not realize what was happening until after the fact.

The following dilemmas are examples of what could go wrong and suggestions for dealing with them. They are true stories, with facts slightly altered to protect the guilty.

Anonymity

I conducted a number of interviews with supervisors at a chemical company in New Jersey. Afterwards, I visited with the Director of Operations to thank him for the cooperation of his department. I shared a few trends and patterns that surfaced in the interviews. The comments were generic in nature, and well within the terms of my verbal contract with the interviewees.

The director asked me to give him a copy of the data I had gathered so that he could be on top of the needs of his employees. I offered him a summary of their comments.

He said he wanted to know what each individual supervisor had said. That would be a violation of my anonymity agreement, so I sidestepped and told him that I did not attach names to the comments, hoping that would deter him.

The director paused and ran his fingers through his hair, then said that he could probably guess who was speaking by issues they brought up and the words they used. He asked for a copy of my notes.

At that point, I had to remind him of our agreement of anonymity. I had not only made a commitment to them, I had received his commitment to it as well. I asked what he really wanted the information for. He admitted he was gathering material to use during performance reviews.

I again offered to give him a summary of my notes. He dropped the subject.

What can you do in a situation like this? Be courteous, remind him of the conditions of your agreement, say what you can do (not what you cannot do), and keep your promises.

Tip	Example
Be courteous	*Thanks for your support today.*
Revisit the conditions of the agreement	*I did promise anonymity.*
Say what you can do	*You are welcome to any data in the summary of my findings that will help you improve the operations of your company.*

Table 8-4. Guidelines for Dealing With Dilemmas During Learner Analysis

Be clear in your mind that your role as a training developer does not include providing information for performance reviews or support for termination proceedings—the reasons most often given for wanting that information.

Politics

Sometimes you might be denied access to the information you need. This could be due to politics, short-handed staff, or contacts who do not have a stake in your success. The personal example that follows is a political one.

A few years ago, I was assigned development of a course for managers of union-member employees that interpreted company policies about attendance, vacations, sick days, overtime, and grievance procedures. My assignment included specific learning objectives.

The learning objective that I was developing content for stated that the learners would be able to explain the grievance process and fill out the associated forms.

The book of procedures, which was available as my key resource, was unclear about the grievance process and included nothing about the forms. Asking around, I found that the subject matter expert on the topic was the union representative. When I told my boss I needed to make an appointment with the union rep, he said that I was not allowed to talk to him, and would have to make my best guess about how the process worked.

It seemed my hands were tied. After interviews with every available manager who had either experience negotiating with the union or who had been a union member, there were gaps in the content. My boss could not fill the gaps, and suggested that I ignore them—let the learners figure it out themselves by experience. Then, I reasoned, what was the point of the learning objective? The learning objective was specific. I could not develop the content to support that objective without speaking to the one person who had that knowledge—the union representative.

I arranged the interview. We met, he explained the process from both management employee and union-member employee sides, and based on the information and examples he gave me, I was able to create job application exercises for the managers.

Course feedback was positive, the application exercises and role plays about the grievance process were praised for their realism, and my boss gave me a diluted version of the lecture I would have received had the content not met its mark.

The choice I made was risky. My friends called it a CLM—career-limiting move. Looking back, I realize there were additional options.

- When someone says no, probe to find out if the restrictions are organizational, the way things have always been done, or personal. The latter two might have no consequences.

- Re-examine the learning objective. If there are not negative consequences for changing the objective (either to the learner or to the project), revise the objective.

- If the objective cannot be changed, try getting referrals from stakeholders to resources that can help you collect content that supports the objective.

- Develop learning objectives after collecting data. (This is the recommended approach that I present in this book.) What the learners need should be the force that shapes objectives.

Inappropriate Roles

Although analysis interviews are conducted for the purpose of training development, opportunistic folks in the company sometimes view the data being collected as a resource. In fact, human resources or other departments that require job or employee information can use much of the same information that you collect.

In addition, your presence at remote locations, headquarters, or other key sites to conduct interviews can be perceived by some as an opportunity to disseminate a message to the people whom you interview.

Think about each role that is imposed upon you that is exterior to your training-related duties. Is the imposed role secondary or inconsequential to your primary role?

How will performing each role affect or delay your training project? Will it require you to perform additional interviews? Will it change the content of your interview? How closely will the data meet their needs? Will sharing the data compromise commitments that you made to those interviewed?

If you are asked to extract information from data that you have collected, then ask how that information will be used. Organizations or managers who wish to save time and money by using training-oriented data, even though it might not be a fit for what they need, should be warned of its limitations. Be aware that part of their expectation might be that the data collector will massage the data to fit the manager's needs—it does happen.

Feel free to accommodate where appropriate, but be careful not to veer from your role in a way that would undermine your mission, or cause people not to trust you or to withhold information from you.

Below are some of the roles that others try to impose on course developers who are planning or conducting data collection. The examples in italics are actual.

A collector of stories about system or individual failures, faults, and weaknesses. This information can be used honorably to improve work conditions or get feedback about a situation, or dishonorably to build a file on individual employees.

I want to know everything that Susan says.   Susan's supervisor

Tell me what people are complaining about.   Department head

A lightning rod for unrelated issues. The key characteristic of a lightning rod is that it attracts and absorbs powerful, typically negative feelings and reactions, thereby diverting interest from other issues. The training developer in this situation could be on the receiving end of complaints, threats, or gossip. On one hand, this role could defuse a potentially negative situation, or on the other hand, it could undermine the data collection process for the project.

The only reason we have to have this training is because the IS Department can't get their act together. What I'd like to tell them is . . .   Operations Manager

You tell those people that if this training doesn't fix them, there is going to be a shakeup.   CEO

An intermediary, to relay a corporate or marketing message to key people—from your organization to the one you are visiting.

You tell them that this is a key initiative. The support for it comes from the very

top, and we are very interested in their success. I expect them to support your development efforts.

Senior Vice President

This product training will make or break the company. Make sure they know that. It's really important. Be sure you tell them that.

Director of Marketing

What If Part of the Overall Problem Is One Person?

Training is intended to enable learners. What if, during the interviews, the same barrier and difficulty keeps coming up, and is attributed to one person—the same person, repeatedly?

If you believe that a change in one person's behavior could improve the operations of the entire organization, pass that information either through your chain of command or through that of the organization you are visiting. There are preliminary actions you should take before doing so, however.

Lay the groundwork, gain support, and assure anonymity. At the end of the interview, say

You are not the only person who named _____ as responsible for making the job more difficult to do. Does management know about this situation? Do you want them to?

or

Several people have named _____ as a key problem in the work environment. I think this is something that management should know about. However, I will not name anyone who made the comments.

How to Observe Job Performance

Observing job performance should be unobtrusive. Observation is appropriate for tasks that are either repetitive or overt. It is not appropriate for tasks that predominantly involve making decisions. In the latter case, you can get more information by sitting with competent job incumbents, and having them explain to you what they are doing and how they make decisions. Flowcharts, Gantt charts, and PERT charts help to define the workflow, as it *should* look, while also identifying areas where problems occur.

Charts provide a handy visual reference, and make it easier for a subject matter expert or master performer to review your results and pinpoint omissions, errors, or misunderstandings.

How to Research Past Performance

Past performance of job incumbents can be a resource for real world applications of skill and knowledge. It can reveal performance behaviors and standards of performance that apply to everyday operations. As with observing at-the-job performance, documents can reveal differences between the way things should be and the way things are in practice.

Documents can reveal differences between the way things should be and the way things are in practice.

Past performance can be gleaned from project progress reports, activity sheets, status reports, project reviews, accounting reports, and other documents that employees and their supervisors complete in the normal course of their jobs.

Documents need not be reports of performance to reveal levels of performance. For example, a pattern of forms with handwritten corrections can indicate a need for instruction about how to use the form, or gaps in knowledge related to the form's content. Of course, the form could be faulty also. Your role as training developer is not to fix the problem. What you can do is alert someone to the problem who can fix it, and prepare training that enables the learner to complete the faulty form with fewer or no errors.

Performance reviews are sometimes considered a resource for performance problems that a target population might have in common. My experience has been that they are seldom specific enough to be useful. If you decide to use them, be sure to work with the Human Resources Department, supervisors, and employees. Get permission from the employees, even if the information you extract will be generic. Legal issues related to viewing performance reviews vary from locale to locale, and should be researched. Make agreements about the scope of your search, and set clear boundaries on how you will use the information.

Look for statements that refer to performance or standards. Your goal is to find statements that indicate what is normal, what is not normal, what can cause or affect detrimental work situations (work ceases in very hot weather, heavy rain can cause delays), skills that need to be developed, and errors, omissions, and situations that were difficult.

Forecasting Learner Analysis Training Tempests

You can tell that stormy weather is forming when these training tempest symptoms appear on the horizon of your training project:

- Employees on your interview list are surprised by your visit or phone call—unaware of the interview.

- You are pressured to reveal your anonymous sources.

- Employees are reluctant to tell you how things really work.

- Management expects training to *fix* the target population.

- Management resists follow up or reinforcement activities to training delivery.

- Supervisors are unable to describe performance criteria—*I'll know it when I see it* mentality.

- Cross-purpose demands undermine effective data collection.

- A group or individual identified for generating problems blames everyone else.

Learner Analysis Summary Report

A summary report encapsulates your major findings about the learners, their attitudes, aptitudes, competencies, knowledge, and skills. It also includes any regional, cultural, environmental, or language considerations that could affect training content or design.

The summary report is intended to provide an overall view of the target training population. You will still need to use the data summary tables and data collection sheets as a resource for detailed information and course content.

Learner Analysis Summary Report

Job Title(s)

This section includes key roles, functions, and features of the job.

Aptitudes

This section includes human qualities and traits that make each task easier to perform. It could include results from established psychological assessments such as the Myers-Briggs Type Indicator.*

Competencies

This section includes abilities that the learner brings to the job that can be used at the job.

Knowledge and Skills

This section includes what the learner needs to know and be able to do, specific to the job and each task. It includes required and used but not required tools, equipment, and aids.

Attitudes

This section includes job tasks and sub-tasks about which the interviewees had very positive or negative feelings, the overall attitude toward each task, and the barriers or obstacles that they perceive in each task, including (mistaken) impressions about what the job should include but does not.

Special Considerations

This section includes any regional, cultural, environmental, or language considerations that could affect training content or design.

Table 8-5. Topics that Should Be Included in a Learner Analysis Summary Report

---

* The most popular model in the world for typing personality styles. Myers-Briggs Type Indicator is a trademark of Consulting Psychologists Press, Inc. See Otto Kroeger and Janet M. Thuesen, *Type Talk: The 16 Personality Types That Determine How We Live, Love and Work* (New York: Delta, 1988), in the Bibliography of References.

Task Analysis

Task analysis is the second of three types of analysis that training development should include. The focus in learner analysis was on the training target population—what they know and are able to do before training. The focus of task analysis is on what a job performer is doing on the job—what the learner must be able to do.

The fundamental purpose of task analysis is to document how to do something. This includes knowledge or skills in the form of procedures and decisions. The results of a task analysis provide content for the training course and indicate appropriate course design and instructional methods.

Task analysis discovers the proficiencies that the learner needs to have. It explicitly identifies, step by step, how tasks are performed. Tasks are processes that include behavior, decisions, or behavior and decisions.

Task analysis includes:

- **Determining major tasks.** You might need to collect information on more tasks than the training will actually cover in order to find out which tasks are important to the training goals, and how tasks relate to one another.

- **Documenting a sequential flow of tasks**, chunked down to the smallest component that the learner needs to know. The smallest component a learner needs to know is determined during data collection.

  For example, for the task of constructing a peanut butter sandwich, your learner analysis might have shown that every member of the training population knows how to twist a lid off a jar and remove bread from its packaging. That means that those activities need not be taught. They are existing competencies. When you record the steps of a task, you can omit steps and instructions for existing competencies.

- **Determining decisions that the performer must make,** the criteria for those decisions, and the next option or task that each decision leads to.

- **Standards of task performance.** Are there time, accuracy, or sequence requirements? What is the range of performance behaviors that are acceptable? What is unacceptable?

- **Constraints and error conditions.** What is forbidden, wrong to do, dangerous? What constitutes an error, what are its consequences, and how can it be corrected? For example, installing a component board into a computer without first grounding yourself is an error condition.

- **Triggering conditions.** Is there an action or event that is required to start the task? For example, an accounting clerk starts a reimbursement task upon receipt of an employee expense voucher.

- **Required interactions with others**, permissions that must be acquired, and reliance on output from other individuals, departments, or organizations. For example, all action on Task 4 stops after Sub-task 4.1.1 until a form signed by the Director of Operations is received.

- **Items required to complete the task**, which include tools, equipment, software, materials, and support services required to complete the task. The tool required for making a peanut butter sandwich is a knife. An emergency back-up tool is a bare finger. A napkin and plate are optional equipment.

The data from task analysis can reveal deficiencies, which are differences between what should be and what actually happens.

In addition, task analysis can reveal bottlenecks caused by deficient skills or knowledge, common prerequisite knowledge and skills, informal processes that supersede formal processes, and abilities or techniques that enhance performance.

What to Do, How to Do It

Of the three types of analysis, task analysis requires you to be the most vigilant and well organized. Your tasks are to ask questions, listen carefully to the answers, ask questions that the answers provoke, observe behavior, record what is happening as it is happening, and be able to recall details in their proper order later as you analyze the data you collected.

How can you do all of this without being swallowed alive by the data?

- **Define the scope of the task analysis.** You might only be observing and collecting data for part of a job: product applications for systems engineers, how to use the new accounting software for accounting clerks, or how to conduct performance reviews for supervisors.

- **Conduct some interviews before observing job performance.** This will give you an overview of what is happening and why. Observe what is happening on the job, record what you see, and create questions about items that need to be clarified, that conflict with what you expected, or that were omitted during the verbal interviews.

Conducting Interviews

Use a form that helps organize the data as you collect it. Illustrate major tasks on paper, easel sheet, or whiteboard as the person you are interviewing speaks, and check for correctness as you go.

This is a give and take process where you will ask questions, ask for clarification, and record answers. The interviewee should do most of the talking. You will probably come back to some points several times as you learn about decisions, performance standards, and other components that add to or change the flow of the task you are discussing.

List major tasks, and write them in behavioral terms, for example, *conduct a pole top rescue, process reimbursement for a travel expense voucher,* or *replace a circuit board.*

Job: Level 4 Electric Power Lineman Apprentice
Major Tasks

1.0 _Conduct a pole top rescue_____

2.0 _____

3.0 _____

4.0 _____

Table 8-6. An Example of How to List Major Job Tasks

If the major tasks are not sequential, but happen independently, list the most frequently done or most important ones first.

Prepare a list of generic questions that you can refer to. After two or three interviews, you will be able to ask questions that are more specific. However, be sure to ask questions in a way that do not lead the interviewee to an answer. Part of the intent of task analysis is to discover what people are actually doing.

Start with the first major task, and ask *What happens first?* Work your way through the questions.

Task Analysis Generic Questions	
Component	**Example Questions**
Major tasks	What are the major tasks (or functions, or duties, or activities) of the job?
Task flow	What happens next? *or* What do you do next?
Decisions	Why do you do that? *or* How do you make that decision? *or* How do you know what to do?
Standards of performance	Does this task (or sub-task) have to be completed within a certain amount of time? With a required degree of accuracy? What level of performance is unacceptable?
Constraints and error conditions	What safety or legal requirements are there? What do they require? What kind of errors or mistakes can happen? What causes them? How often do they occur? How serious are they? What are the consequences? How are they fixed? Please describe an example.
Trigger conditions	What happens first? *or* What is the first thing you do? *or* What action triggers this task for you?
Required interactions	Who do you have to talk with, submit work to, ask for permission from, or get something from, to move forward with this task or sub-task? What part of this task can be delayed or stopped by someone else?
Required items	What kind of support items do you need to perform this task? (This includes tools, equipment, software, materials, or support services.)

Table 8-7. Questions That Help Define Each Job Task

Record each of the sub-tasks on a separate line. Write them in action terms—what the performer does. Leave space between them so that later you can easily insert steps that were overlooked or notes about constraints, errors, and other important items that might relate to that sub-task.

Job: **Level 4 Electric Power Lineman Apprentice**

Major Tasks:

1.0 Conduct a pole top rescue

2.0 Install distribution transformers

3.0 Assist journeymen power linemen

4.0 Maintain energized lines

1.0　　Conduct a pole top rescue

　　1.1　　Recognize that someone needs help

　　　　1.1.1　　See or hear a warning event, such as a flashover or explosion

　　　　1.1.2　　Shout to crew member—does not answer, seems dazed or stunned

　　1.2　　Put on personal protection gear—rubber gloves and sleeves. Note: speed and safety are critical elements

　　1.3　　Assess situation

　　　　1.3.1　　Physical condition of pole

　　　　1.3.2　　Live line tool

　　　　1.3.3　　Need for extra rubber goods

　　　　1.3.4　　Condition of hand-line on pole

　　1.4　　Climb to rescue position, just above the injured person

　　　　1.4.1　　Determine the injured person's condition

　　　　1.4.2　　Conscious

　　　　1.4.3　　Unconscious, breathing

　　　　1.4.4　　Unconscious, not breathing

　　　　1.4.5　　Unconscious, not breathing, heart stopped

Table 8-8. Example of Sub-tasks for Task 1.0

Task Flowcharting

Flowcharting helps you decide to what level to chunk down a task, and how to make sense of it. Drawing a flowchart of a task can help you understand what the data is telling you, will omit information that is not germane to the task, and will help the people you interviewed check the correctness and completeness of what you have recorded.

Task analysis includes collecting data and mapping the flow of it. The order in which you perform these two operations depends on the complexity of the tasks. It would be unusual for you to get everything you need the first time through the flowcharting process or the task description process. Steps are always missed. Decisions, tools, or constraints can be overlooked. Expect to go back and forth between collecting data and charting the flow of activities, between asking questions and updating the data several, if not many, times.

A guideline for how much detail to include in the flowchart is to ask if the sub-task requires instruction. If the answer is no, the learner has prerequisite knowledge required for the sub-task; you have chunked down far enough and those sub-task steps do not need to be added to the flowchart.

There are two major types of flowcharts used in task analysis: procedural and hierarchical. A flowchart can also be a combination of procedural and hierarchical. The type of flowchart called for is based on the tasks being analyzed.

A procedural flowchart is appropriate to use when the tasks and sub-tasks are related to one another, and can be represented one after the other, in a linear manner. The sub-tasks do not require additional instruction.

This flowchart represents a procedural task called *making a peanut butter sandwich*. It illustrates linear relationships, where Sub-task 1 leads to Sub-task 2, then Sub-task 3. Each sub-task can be performed without additional instruction, even though additional instruction is possible.

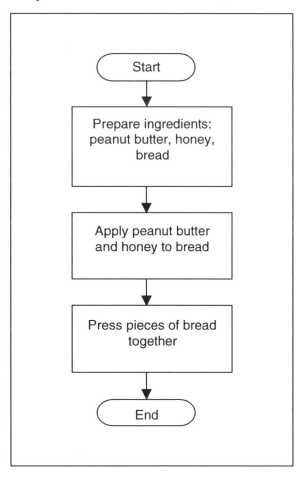

Table 8-9. Flowchart for a Simple Linear Task—Making a Peanut Butter Sandwich

Complex task flows should be represented by a hierarchical task analysis. The relationships among sub-tasks are not linear, and the sub-tasks require instruction. Hierarchical relationships indicate conditions that lead to the next step.

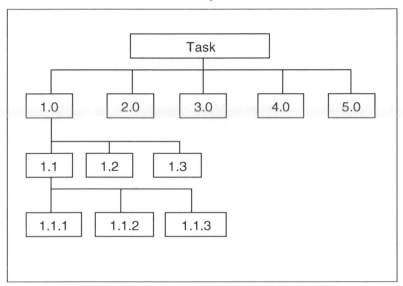

Table 8-10. Example of Hierarchical Task Analysis Flowchart

A task analysis flowchart can include a combination of procedural and hierarchical flowcharting.

The flowchart is a tool for clarifying how to perform a task. If you find that the format is too constraining for the tasks you are analyzing, add components that will reflect the information you need to display, for example, decisions and overlapping tasks. Alternative ways of graphically displaying tasks and sub-tasks are discussed in the section called *Other Helpful Charting Methods*.

Other Helpful Charting Methods

PERT charts illustrate the interdependence of tasks, and could be helpful with very complex tasks, or where more than one task is done at a time. This PERT chart has numbers in each icon, which serve as reference names for each sub-task. The icon can be some other shape than a circle, and can contain whatever information you need.

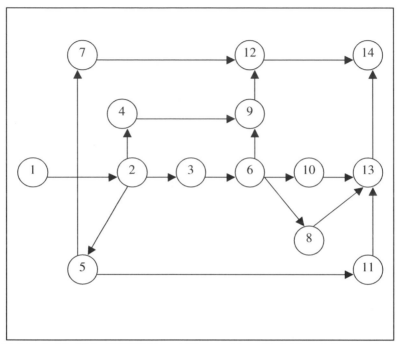

Table 8-11. This PERT Chart Shows How Relationships and Complex Tasks Can Be Illustrated

For example, the PERT chart icon on the following page is similar to those generated by Microsoft Project 98 software. It includes task name, task number, how long the task takes to complete, the equipment required to perform the task, and task performance standards.

Task Name	
Task number	Duration of task
Required items	Performance standards

Table 8-12. Enlarged Format for a Generic Informative PERT Chart Icon

Completed, it could look like the following example. This type of informational icon could be inserted in place of each numbered circle in the preceding PERT chart example.

Set Pole	
Task 3.0	2 hours
Backhoe, bucket truck, lineman tools, safety equipment	Standards: line tension within company standards, no bow in pole

Table 8-13. Example of a Completed Informative PERT Chart Icon

Decision charts are another helpful way to map options. A decision chart presents each decision as a question that can be answered with *yes* or *no*. If there are several options, there will be several yes or no decisions in a row. The next example demonstrates this method.

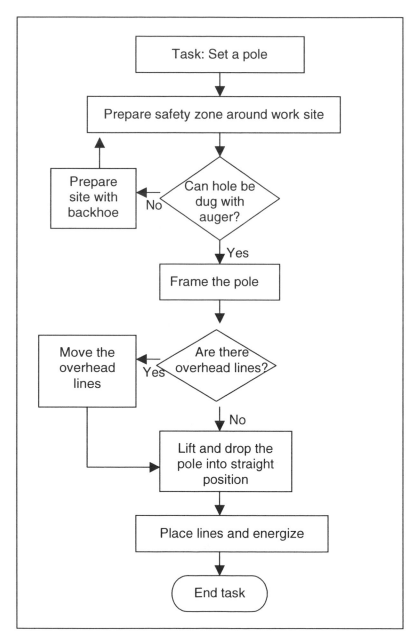

Table 8-14. Example Decision Chart

Verification Issues

The help you receive from subject matter experts should include:

- Deciding what task behaviors are stylistic to individuals

- Substantiating which sub-tasks contribute to the task, and which are optional

- Ensuring that each important step and decision has been included, and that they are in the right order

- Ensuring that priorities, standards, error conditions, and required items are included wherever they are required within a task

Ensure That Only Key Content Is Included

Ensure that only key content is included in your course by asking these questions for each task and sub-task in your task analysis:

- Does this sub-task have safety or legal implications?

- For sub-tasks that do not have safety or legal implications, rate them according to the following criteria:

  - **Criticality.** What would happen if this task were not done? How willing are we to take the risk?

  - **Accuracy.** What would happen if this task were not performed correctly? What degree of accuracy is acceptable? Desirable?

  - **Frequency.** How often is this task performed? Daily, weekly, or monthly?

  - **Complexity.** How difficult is this task to learn? Master? How much practice and coaching does it require?

Forecasting Task Analysis Training Tempests

You can tell that stormy weather is forming when these training tempest symptoms appear on the horizon of your training project:

- Barriers to communicating with current job performers or subject matter experts

- Pressure to skip analysis and move into content development

- Believing that *best guesses* about task components are as good as collecting data

Training Environment Analysis

The purpose of the training environment analysis is to identify the conditions under which training will occur, how the course will be introduced into the system, and how the training process will be managed. It is the third of three types of analysis a training development process should include. Its focus is on enabling training implementation. This type of analysis is sometimes called context analysis.

A training environment analysis is important because the training delivery opportunities and constraints it identifies will influence your content design and choice of instructional methods.

You can more easily answer questions about the training environment after completing the learner and task analyses. The data collected from them can help you make basic decisions, such as whether the course design should include classroom or non-classroom components, monitored or self-paced instruction, and whether the delivery methods should include instructors, computers, or hands-on aids. Additional instructional method and design decisions are variations of these.

How to Do It

Conditions that should be included in the training environment analysis are:

- **Physical environment.** Environment includes the location of the training and its facilities. An indoor environment can include a meeting room, breakout rooms, power, climate control, computer power and networking facilities, rest rooms, dining facilities, and catering services. The environment section needs to answer questions such as:

  - How will access to the corporate intranet be established from a hotel meeting room?

- Will instruction be conducted in a manhole, in an aircraft simulator, on a vessel at sea, in a foreign country?

- **Limitations**. This section of the analysis describes limitations regarding scheduling, facilities, cost, equipment, instructors, or other essential element that will affect the success of course delivery. Addressing this condition determines whether what you need will be available when you need it.

- **Introduction and integration**. This section of the analysis describes how the course will be introduced and integrated into the existing training curriculum or corporate process.

- **Equipment and media availability**. This section describes the equipment and media that are required for course development and delivery.

- **Prerequisites**. This section describes what licenses, certifications, completed courses, or experience the learner must have before taking this course. It includes how prerequisites will be monitored, and what consequences there will be for not satisfying them.

- **Enrollment conditions**. This section describes requirements that encourage or discourage a learner from enrolling. Incentives include mandatory enrollment and freedom from completing routine job requirements during training dates. Disincentives include weekend travel, class on Saturday, and job requirements and deadlines that must be met despite training. Enrollment conditions also include prerequisites, how they will be monitored, and the consequences for enrolling without them.

- **Course enrollment and completion procedures**. This section includes the steps that must be taken to enroll and record a learner's completion of the course.

- **Evaluation and verification**. This section describes how the learning will be evaluated, including testing, grading, and reporting. Verification describes how evaluated performance will be proven, for example, by certificate, by appearance on a roster of specially qualified personnel, by inclusion in a database, or by issuance of a card to carry personally.

Forecasting Training Environment Analysis Training Tempests

You can tell that stormy weather is forming when these training tempest symptoms appear on the horizon of your training project:

- Stakeholders resist committing the equipment and facilities your course requires, despite their inclusion in the signed project plan.

- You are encouraged to "make do" or "work around" the absence of required equipment or facilities.

- Enrollment conditions or prerequisite activities are dismissed as frivolous.

Training Environment Analysis		
Condition	**Questions to Ask**	**Sample Answers**
Physical environment	Will a classroom be available in the simulator building during the time that the simulator is available?	During the fourth weeks of March, April, June, and October the Boeing 747 simulator and a classroom are both available.
Limitations	What time, cost, scheduling, instructor, facility, or other limitations are there?	Simulator. The Boeing 747 simulator is closed for maintenance December 20-29. Reservations need to be four months in advance. Equipment. Intranet connections will only be a problem in the eastern region. Will need to contract with an outside vendor for T1 connection and physical link services. First-choice instructors are available for the pilot delivery but not for the next six months.
Introduction, integration	How will the course will be introduced and integrated into the existing training curriculum, corporate system?	The pilot delivery of the course will be conducted at Boeing Field in Seattle, and then rolled out to regional sites over a period of 12 months. The course will be reviewed quarterly and updated as needed. It will be revised yearly. Funding for revisions will be a jet operations line item.
Equipment, media availability	What equipment will be required for course development? Course delivery?	The development team needs access to the simulator for three weeks in January, and access to supporting documentation from January through March.

Table 8-15. Guidelines for Performing a Training Environment Analysis

Training Environment Analysis, continued

Condition	Questions to Ask	Sample Answers
Prerequisites	What prerequisites will the learner have? How will this be monitored? What are the consequences for not satisfying them?	Prerequisite. A large commercial aircraft pilot's license, that is active and in good standing Monitored. The training review board will hand-select training candidates. Consequences. No one will be considered as a candidate for training without it. There will be no exceptions.
Enrollment conditions	By what method will training seats be filled? Will training require working at times other than 9-5 Monday through Friday, or travel?	Enrollment. All of the candidates the first year will be invited to training. After that, self-nominated candidates will be considered for unfilled seats on a waiting list basis. Shifts. Courses will be held during normal work hours and may require weekend travel.
Course completion procedures	What are the steps for enrollment? How will course completion or non-completion be reported? Where will a record of completion be retained? To whom will it be sent? How can a copy be requested?	The training review board will submit each course roster to the headquarters scheduling office when 75% of the seats have been registered. Remaining seats will be filled on a per candidate basis by approved referrals from the review board.

Table 8-15, continued. Guidelines for Performing a Training Environment Analysis

Training Environment Analysis, continued

Condition	Questions to Ask	Sample Answers
Evaluation and verification	How will learning be evaluated? How will successful completion of the course be certified?	Evaluation. Each candidate must pass a written exam, a verbal exam, and a simulation exercise with a minimum score for each of 90%. Verification. Passing candidates will be listed on a database of certified Boeing 747 pilots and receive a personal certificate of achievement.

Table 8-15, continued. Guidelines for Performing a Training Environment Analysis

How to Organize Your Notes

Data collection means creating many records. Whether paper-based or computer-based, you will need a system for organizing your notes.

If you filled out a separate form for each interviewee, there might have been overflow to the back of the page, or onto separate sheets of paper. Make sure that each overflow comment is preceded by the number of the question that it answers. For example, comments related to question 1 could be numbered 1.1, 1.2, and 1.3. If the question has parts *a* and *b*, the numbering would become 1a.1, 1a.2, 1a.3, 1b.1, 1b.2, 1b.3.

I have sorted comments in a number of ways. What works best depends on the data itself. If all comments related to a single question are grouped together, patterns and trends related to that question can surface.

Being able to see patterns and trends for individuals can help determine if there are subgroups of learners that training content needs to target. If you want to be aware of relationships, patterns, and trends among questions from a single respondent (for example, to be able to see that the answer to Question 4 was always *blue* whenever the answer to Question 1 was *round*), then you will need to keep answers from individual respondents related to each other. You can add an additional code to the numbering system that relates to location and assigns a number to each set of answers. For example, answers to Question 1 from respondent three from the Denver plant could be DP3.1.1.

Binders can keep things in order, and so can heavy-duty clips (the black ones with handles). Bound books such as composition books keep pages together if you do not need to rearrange sections or pages.

A matrix can help cross-reference data if the data indicate categories into which you can group answers.

Experience at the Job			
Less than 2 months	2-6 months	6 months to one year	More than one year
Question 1			
Question 2			
Question 3			

Table 8-16. Example of a Cross-Reference Matrix

Analysis Report

The analysis report is a summary of key findings from each analysis. It includes your recommendations for instructional design, media use, and implementation requirements. It should list the major components of the course, and your estimate of the time it will take to develop them.

If some items in the analysis report seem like duplications of items in the project plan, they are not. They are updates of the plan, based now on hard data, which will help you make content and design decisions.

For example, the analysis might have revealed that most of the training population is more computer literate than you expected, so course components that address basic computer skills training could be omitted, saving development time and money.

Step 3—Objectives

Objectives are statements that focus course content. They support task performance. They should specify what behavior changes will result from training, and directly relate course content to task competencies.

A sound objective is verifiable—it can be measured via exam, simulation, checklist, or monitored activities. Verification methods are also called tests because they test for what learning has occurred.

Why Many Courses Fail

Poorly developed objectives are largely responsible for ineffective instruction because content hangs upon a framework of objectives. Pull out the workbook for a course you have taken and look for the objectives. How clearly do they state what you will walk away from the course knowing or being able to do? Do the objectives include performance, conditions, or standards? Is the stated objective really a course goal? How much of the course is presented as entertainment? Plays on your emotion?

Courses that promise emotional rewards—that you will become more friendly, promotable, or expert—or that promise you will be entertained, might be using unverifiable claims to conceal an absence of substantive content.

Test Items Depend on Objectives

Test items should parallel performance objectives: they should verify competencies that are defined by the objectives. How to develop criterion tests will be covered in the next chapter.

Your task at this step of training development is to create behavioral targets for the learner to reach by the end of the training course. Well-constructed objectives lead to reliable tests. They in turn lead to solid design and course content decisions. The result is a course that makes a difference in performance.

Components of Objectives

Objectives have three components. All three should be included in each objective you write.

- **Performance**. Performance is what the learner will be able to do as a result of training. A commonly used beginning to a performance statement is *the learner will be able to.* The performance should be in behavioral terms. Facilitate this by using action verbs such as describe, perform, and count. A list of performance verbs is included in this chapter.

- **Conditions.** Conditions are the circumstances under which performance will occur, for example, *during role-play, using job aids, with thirty minutes to research the Internet, under simulated work conditions,* or *while being observed.* Make every effort to design performance conditions that align with or match real-world performance.

- **Standards.** Standards describe how well the learner will be expected to perform each objective, for example, *with 80%*

accuracy, or *with a minimum rating of satisfactory for each category.*

The absence or poor construction of any of these components weakens the effectiveness and verifiability of the objective.

Exceptions to Using Behavioral Objectives

I am unable to think of an exception to using behavioral objectives. If training is to make a difference, changes need to be observable—something you can detect with the senses. Even a course that focuses on attitudes can have verifiable objectives. For example, a cultural diversity course creates awareness of attitudes and encourages acceptance of differences. Verifiable activities can include opinion surveys, role-play about culturally sensitive issues, and tests about course content. None of these activities need to force a point of view on the learner. Objectives can be to enable the learner to describe his point of view, describe other points of view, and role-play other points of view.

Course Objective

The course objective is a statement that includes all three components of an objective—performance, conditions, and standards. A properly written course objective, although it can be cumbersome, will tell you exactly what the course is intended to deliver. We can use the workshop on which this book is based as an example:

By the end of this workshop, the learner will have developed a module for an example training project using the eight-step training development process, and any checklists, guides, or templates in the workbook.

A well-written course objective directly relates to course content. Objectives for each smaller unit of learning should support the objective above it in the hierarchy.

Course Goal

The course objective is not the same as the course goal. The course goal, which was included in the project plan, states the purpose of the course. It is not intended to define what the learner will be able to do as a result of training. The course goal for the workshop mentioned above is: *to enable technical writers to develop an effective training course.*

Perhaps you are wondering why that statement cannot be used as an objective. It is not an objective because all three required components are missing: It states that it will enable the learner, but does not state what the learner's performance will be. It does not include conditions or standards. *Effective* is subjective —it cannot be verified.

The course goal does not take the place of a course objective, but it does focus managers, team members, and subject matter experts on the desired effect of the course.

Levels of Objectives

Course objective. There is one course objective. All other objectives are subordinate to it.

Content objectives. There should be at least one objective for each content unit. Content might be divided into modules, chapters, and lessons. Each content unit should have objectives that support it, and that directly relate to the objective to which it is subordinate. Each subordinate level is more content specific than the level above it.

Course objective: By the end of the course, the learner will be able to present a sales presentation that includes system solutions for enterprise customers.

Module 1 objective: By the end of Module 1, the learner will be able to describe key product solutions for enterprise customers.

Module 1, Chapter 1 objective: By the end of Chapter 1, the learner will be able to name the benefits and features of virtual private network product solutions for enterprise customers with 80% accuracy.

Module 1, Chapter 2 objectives: By the end of Chapter 2, the learner will be able to: (a) name the benefits and features of local area network (LAN) product solutions for enterprise customers with 80% accuracy, and (b) draw a LAN architecture for a three-building campus using a whiteboard, given the business needs of a sample customer.

Module 2 objective: By the end of Module 2, the learner will be able to present a 20-minute sales presentation in a role-play situation that includes a product solution for an example customer.

Scope

It is important to remember that objectives apply only to the duration of the course. The goal of a course is not to teach mastery, but to enable—to prepare, direct, and coach.

Sometimes stakeholders expect a training course to *fix* the learner—that, for example, customer complaints will dramatically drop after a customer service training course. Sometimes training is not the solution—a distribution process or product quality problem is something that training cannot correct.

Sometimes training is only part of an intervention. Organizational changes might be required in addition to training.

Learners might expect to solve their immediate problems in the course of the training. Some can. Some have unrealistic expectations. Recently, a product account manager, hired two weeks before, told me that he expected the four-day product course he was attending to prepare him for a multi-million dollar account sales presentation the next week. His expectation was optimistic but unrealistic. His time might have been better spent pulling together a support team of experienced large account colleagues to prepare a product solution, then plan, prepare, and practice their presentation.

Verifiable Verbs Focus Objectives

Verifiable verbs breathe life into objectives by describing action. The action of each objective is what determines whether you can verify it. The following tables provide examples of verifiable and unverifiable verbs.

Verifiable Verbs				
Choose	Select	Rate	Develop	Challenge
Contrast	Indicate	Criticize	Create	Solve
Define	Show	Distinguish	Do	Judge
Describe	Tell	Predict	Make	Match
Omit	Translate	Identify	Plan	Operate
Restate	Classify	Appraise	Choose	Defend
Schedule	Explain	Compare	Compose	Design

Commonly Used Unverifiable Verbs			
Appreciate	Enjoy	Learn	Rehearse
Be aware of	Know	Like	Think about
Comprehend	Know how to	Practice	Understand

Table 9-1. The Examples in the Two Tables Above Illustrate That Verifiable Actions Can Be Observed and Tested, Whereas Unverifiable Actions Cannot Be

To demonstrate how the action of each verb determines whether you can verify it, take a quick quiz. Which of the following statements are verifiable? Answers are in the footnote following the statements.

1. By the end of this module, the learner will be able to describe the five-step process.

2. By the end of this module, the learner will know how to attach dry wall to bare wood.

3. During this course, the participant will learn about four products used by financial accounts customers.

4. By the end of this chapter, the learner will be able to calculate the circumference of a circle.

5. By the end of this module, the learner will be aware of three warning signs of an allergic reaction to penicillin.*

You might be surprised that objectives that include performance, conditions, and standards could be ineffective. Nevertheless, it is true. If the action is inside someone's head, the performance component of the objective is not verifiable. Learning can only be tested if it can be verified by the senses.

Objectives can be verified by activities such as those named in this table.

Verification Activities	
• Checklist	• Quiz
• Demonstration	• Role Play
• Exam	• Simulation
• Presentation	

Table 9-2. Activities That Facilitate Performance Objectives

Real-Life Example

The following example illustrates an objective with many enabling objectives. Enabling objectives support the objective to which they are subordinate. The following objective would be easy to test using a checklist format because all of the performance requirements are the same for each item. Simply add a check box before each item the examiner is to check off, and add a space for comments.

For each of the following substation equipment items, the learner will be able to:

• Identify it.

• Describe its purpose.

---

*Quiz Answers: 1 and 4 are verifiable. They use testable verbs such as describe, calculate. Verbs such as know, learn, and be aware of are not testable.

- Correctly assess its status.

- Use, operate, or replace it, as appropriate.

Substation Equipment Items

Air circuit breakers	Grounding transformers	Bus support insulators	Metal-clad switchgear
Manholes	Capacitors	Meters	Microwave
Circuit switchers	Concrete foundations	Oil circuit breakers	Potential transformers
Conduits	Control House	Potheads	Power transformers
Control panels	Control wires	Relays	Supervisory control
Coupling capacitors	Current transformers	Power-line carrier batteries	SF_6 circuit breakers
Disconnect switches	Duct runs	Steel super-structures	Shunt reactors
Frequency changers	Grounding resistors	Rectifiers	Suspension insulators
Battery chargers	High-voltage cables	Synchronous condensers	Vacuum circuit breakers
High-voltage fuses	Lightning arresters	Manholes	Metal-clad switchgear

Levels of Learner Expertise

Objectives should match the target population's level of expertise. The data that you collected in the analysis step should provide a clear indication of what they need to know. Use the following categories to group the skill and knowledge level of your learners.

Entry Level. At this level the learner has no experience and is unaware of what he does not know. For example, a person who wants to go canoeing for the first time is probably aware that he will need to pull a paddle through water to move a boat. But he is unaware that paddling includes stroke techniques such as insertion, compression, and return, or that he must learn about steering, boat balance, and safety.

Novice. At this level the learner is aware that he does not know and may or may not be aware of what he does not know. At this level, the learner has some experience but little knowledge or few skills. For example, a novice canoeist can make his boat travel from one shore to another, but not in a straight line. He knows that he needs to improve stroke and steering skills. The learner in this situation is aware that there is a problem he can learn to solve and cognitively knows what his goal is, but is unable to perform at a proficient level.

Experienced. At this level the learner has achieved a level of expertise, but requires practice, help, or support to improve skills and knowledge. The learner knows what he knows, and works at it.

Expert. At this level the learner demonstrates expertise, but cannot always describe what he knows, how he makes decisions, or how he does what he does. Expertise is at an unconscious level. The learner has a wide range of knowledge, a deep level of skills, and can demonstrate them without conscious effort.

Overview of Bloom's Taxonomy

A system of classifying intellectual behavior that is important to learning was developed almost fifty years ago by a group of educational psychologists led by Benjamin Bloom. Bloom's taxonomy* has become widely known in the training and development community. It provides a reasonable framework for technical communicators to use when deciding which training components will add value to documentation.

The taxonomy—a way of organizing things into distinct areas—has three categories, which overlap. They are cognitive, affective, and psychomotor. Each category can be triggered by specific

---

* Benjamin S. Bloom, Taxonomy of Educational Objectives: The Classification of Educational Goals (London: Longman Group, 1969).

activities. Verbs related to those activities are included with the description of each category.

Cognitive learning has to do with factual knowledge. It includes six progressively complex levels of knowledge. Cognitive learning is the category within which most training courses are developed.

- *Knowledge.* Defined as recalling or recognizing facts. Verbs that indicate learning at this level include: arrange, define, duplicate, label, list, memorize, name, order, recognize, relate, recall, repeat, reproduce, and state.

- *Comprehension.* Defined as understanding relationships and meanings. Verbs that indicate learning at this level include: classify, describe, discuss, explain, express, identify, indicate, locate, recognize, report, restate, review, select, and translate.

- *Application.* Defined as being able to appropriately apply solutions to unfamiliar situations. Verbs that indicate learning at this level include: apply, choose, demonstrate, dramatize, employ, illustrate, interpret, operate, practice, schedule, sketch, solve, use, and write.

- *Analysis.* Defined as being able to separate a situation into its constituent parts. Verbs that indicate learning at this level include: analyze, appraise, calculate, categorize, compare, contrast, criticize, differentiate, discriminate, distinguish, examine, experiment, question, and test.

- *Synthesis.* Defined as being able to combine elements to form a whole. Verbs that indicate learning at this level include: arrange, assemble, collect, compose, construct, create, design, develop, formulate, manage, organize, plan, prepare, propose, set up, and write.

- *Evaluation.* Defined as the ability to appraise the value of something—a subjective ability. Verbs that indicate learning at this level include: argue, assess, attach, choose, compare, defend, estimate, evaluate, judge, predict, rate, select, support, and value.

Affective learning arouses feelings and emotions. It is demonstrated by behaviors that indicate attitudes, awareness, interest, attention, concern, and responsibility. Verbs that indicate learning at this level include: accept, attempt, challenge, defend, dispute, join, judge, praise, question, share, support, and volunteer.

Psychomotor learning requires physical action combined with thought, for example, using tools, dancing, or performing athletically. Verbs and phrases that indicate learning at this level include: bend, grasp, handle, operate, reach, shorten, stretch, discern by touch, and communicate using hand signals.

Real-Life Consequence

The example that follows is a real-life situation that demonstrates the importance of following a systematic approach to developing training.

My consulting assignment was to assess an existing two-year training curriculum for power dispatchers in the electrical energy industry, and recommend ways to make it more effective.

The most important finding was that the goal of the two-year program did not match what the program was designed to deliver. The stated goal was to prepare the learner to perform a system power dispatcher's job, specifically generation system dispatching. However, there were two levels of dispatchers. One handled transmission and distribution, and the other generation, the latter being the more advanced level. The curriculum content, at-the-job training activities, and competency tests prepared the program graduate for transmission and distribution systems dispatching. There was an important gap between intent and reality.

A collision of factors was responsible for this situation, which includes: recent down-sizing that stripped the company of experienced people to fill key positions, pressure to get a training program into the field, trying to pull together a training program from existing materials without determining their fit, and not taking time to define the problem and determine whether the proposed solution would solve it.

How to Forecast Training Tempests

Stormy training development weather is forecast by any of the objectives-related symptoms below:

- Objectives are developed after the course content is developed.

- Objectives do not correlate with the course goal, analysis results, or content.

- Objectives are written to mastery level performance standards.

- Objectives do not match the expertise level of the learners.

- Objectives are not verifiable.

Step 4—Criterion Tests

A criterion is a standard on which a judgment can be based. Criterion tests assess learning, and are based on course objectives. They test whether the learner can demonstrate the knowledge or skills described in the objectives.

The points you need to remember when developing test items and planning the administration of tests are outlined in this chapter.

Create Test Items Before Content

Objectives project what the learning outcome will be. Tests evaluate whether the learning objectives were met. Criterion tests and objectives together provide a skeletal structure on which to build the course content, which includes the selection of instructional methods that best supports the content, the selection of instructional media that best supports the instructional methodology, and the documentation, such as learner and instructor guides, that best facilitates the content.

Guidelines for Sound Test Design

Test content should not surprise the learner. The content and level of difficulty should parallel the content of the training course, which should parallel what they will face on the job.

Mastery is not the goal. Even a bomb-defusing course is not expected to result in mastery. How confident would you feel that you could defuse bombs without supervision or error after reading a manual, seeing a film, listening to lectures, and working with simulations? Skill and judgment-dependent tasks also require observing experienced task performers and performing the task with coaching. Coaching, drill, practice, feedback, and reinforcement activities should be based on the learner's level of expertise, with the goal being to bring the learner to the next level of expertise.

Sound objectives lead to sound test items. Test items are easier to design if they are based on verifiable objectives. This step will move more quickly if the objectives were properly developed. If you find yourself unable to correlate test items with objectives, then you might need to rewrite the objectives or reconsider what you are testing.

Challenge the learner. Include test items with different levels of difficulty. If the intellectual level of the course is cognitive, for example, then include items that test on an analysis level as well as on a knowledge level.

Objectives drive the form of the test. If an objective states that the learner will be able to splice a fiber-optic cable, then testing should include doing that. Describing the cable splicing process does not test the objective.

Determine how the test will be used. Another determinant of test content is how its results will be used. The content—what goes into the test; its format—what kind of test it will be; and its duration—how long and complex the test will be, can all be related to the application of the test results. Will it provide a benchmark for the learner at mid-course? Will it certify the ability of the learner to perform specialized tasks? Will it determine entry into an elite group?

How to Ensure Proper Test Content

Use the following two questions to ensure that the right content is included in a test.

* Is each learning objective addressed by at least one test question?

* Does each test question relate to a specific learning objective?

Determine Test Features and Administration

Use the following list of questions to determine what features are most appropriate for the test, and to plan for its administration.

* **What is the intent of the test?** The answer to this question helps determine how long and difficult the test should be. It can also indicate whether the test process needs to be controlled, for example, by a requirement for monitors or by a prohibition against collaboration among the test-takers.

  Common reasons for testing are to:

  – Establish qualification

  – Determine readiness for promotion

  – Provide a benchmark for improvement

  – Provide an indicator of performance

  – Provide a self-assessment for the learner

  – Evaluate performance in real-life situations

* **At what level of expertise is the learner**—entry level, novice, experienced, or expert?

* Will the test be electronically generated?

- Will it be created from a pool of questions? If so, then you will need to develop more questions than are required for one test.

- What are the selection criteria? For example, will the software select every fourth question? Two questions for every objective? The answer to this question will determine how you format and organize the test. Administrative guidelines will also be required for the instructor and test administrator.

- **How will the results of the test be used**? Your answer can help determine, among other things, whether to produce certificates, develop a database, and prepare letters for reporting test results. Each of these requires administrative support. A plan describing that requirement should be part of your design document. Test results can be used:

  - As reference in performance reviews

  - To submit to certifying agencies as evidence of competence

  - To establish prerequisite ability for the next level of job performance or training

  - To prove a course completion requirement

- **What level of learning must be proven**? For example, if the learner needs only to be able to recall facts, then multiple choice, fill in the blank, and matching are appropriate indicators. If the learner has to prove competency in a skill that involves complex thought processes and decisions, then require a written plan, a rationale for the plan, and a demonstration of the skills. If the objectives are well written, they can indicate the intellectual level that should be tested. Refer to the overview of Bloom's taxonomy in the chapter on objectives for a guideline of words to use for each intellectual level of learning.

- **What degree of verifiability must be proven**? If the learner has to perform a task that requires complex thought processes that are not visible, and if the thought process is important, require that all calculations, research, and notes be documented. The test environment would need to support that requirement, for example, by providing bound composition books.

Tips and Techniques for Test Construction

The following are general guidelines for writing tests.

- Relate each test item to an objective.

- Avoid double negatives, such as It is not true that robins do not sing after dark.

- Avoid ambiguous or tricky wording.

- Ensure that there is only one correct answer.

- Avoid multiple-choice answer groupings that minimize choices and include answers like the one below:

    What color is the sky?

    a.   Red

    b.   Green

    c.   Red and green

    d.   Neither red nor green

    e.   None of the above

    A better question would be:

    What color is the sky?

    a.   Red

    b.   Blue

    c.   Green

    d.   Yellow

- If there is not enough content to create multiple-choice answers, chose another format such as true/false or matching.

    True or False? The sky is red.

- Ensure that the test items are independent of one another—that they neither give clues to answers in other questions nor depend upon information from one question to get a correct answer in another.

- Include instructions with each category of questions. Because of international, cultural, and educational diversity, you cannot assume that the test-takers will know what to do.

- Include instructions for the learner regarding how the test will be graded, what score is passing, and whether it is better to guess at unknown answers or leave them blank.

Determine Test Duration

How long and complex a test should be depends on its intent. Competency certification for a network engineer will be more rigorous and time consuming than a quiz to reinforce new hire course content.

Following are cases that are examples of test development situations. Test yourself by reading the case and considering what you would do. The answer follows each case.

Case 1. The Human Resources department offers a new hire course that lasts two days and is intended to establish a foundation level of knowledge about the company, its mission, what forms to fill out, procedures to be aware of, reporting hierarchy, e-mail and computer support services, and company benefits. What are your recommendations for test format, content, and duration?

Answer. The intent is not to evaluate the learner, but to assist him or her. The goal of the exam is to highlight points of value to the learner and reinforce where to find answers to questions a learner might have after the course. The exam should be short: it should take about fifteen minutes to complete. Ask questions that require recall, such as matching, multiple choice, and short answer. Make the exam open book.

Case 2. A certification course—similar to those offered by Microsoft and Cisco Systems, which attest to expertness about a specialized body of knowledge—that stretches over several weeks and requires hours of self-study. It includes exams that cover increments of learning as well as a final certification exam. What should the final exam include?

Answer. The intent of the final exam is to guarantee that the learner has a working level of knowledge about a specific body of knowledge, for example, Cisco routers. Create a test that includes all key topics, and difficulty levels from basic to complex. Include factual recall, analysis, synthesis, and application questions such as diagnosis, recommendations, and problem resolution. The exam should be long enough to test each major topic of the course, and could last several hours. There may need to be a verbal component and a demonstration component, depending upon the nature of the certification.

Case 3. An elite military group wants to develop training that will prepare those who pass it for the rigors of duty. It needs to include mental and physical components, as well as developing teamwork.

Answer. The intent of an elite group basic training course, such as SEAL training, is not only to develop a specialized set of skills, but also to weed out the able from the unable, to test extremes of knowledge and skills, assess the ability to persevere, and to develop teamwork while working at extreme fringes of ability and mental strength. Testing might include a paper-based component, but will rely heavily on situational scenarios that require analysis-level thinking (separating a situation into parts), synthesis-level thinking (combining elements to form a whole), and decisive action-thinking under a number of constraints, challenges, and distractions that closely resemble scenarios in the field.

The following table provides an example of how a test evolves from a performance objective.

Performance objective:	Tests what:	Based on results of the test, the learner will:	How the learner will be tested:
Be able to splice fiber-optic cable using appropriate tools and company procedures that results in 100% transmission accuracy on 80% of attempts in job-like settings.	Performance Procedure Quality Accuracy Skill in a simulated setting	If passes, be promoted to Step 2 of the telephone installer apprentice program. If fails, will repeat Weeks 5-9 of Step 1 training.	A qualified journeyman installer will observe and evaluate as the learner splices five fiber-optic cables: two underground, and three in connector boxes.
Be able to deliver a 30-minute customer product presentation to an audience of peers that identifies a simulated customer problem, proposes how selected products provide a solution, and makes a purchase recommendation.	Knowledge Application Analysis Synthesis Skill in role play setting	Be able to identify customer problems, select products that provide a solution, and make purchase recommendations.	In a classroom, the learner will prepare and present a product presentation, which will be videotaped. Peers and the instructor, all of whom will be using an evaluation checklist that focuses on content and strategy, will evaluate learners.

Table 10-1. How a Test Item Evolves from a Performance Objective

This table correlates learning outcomes with appropriate test strategies, using terms that relate to the intellectual levels described in Bloom's taxonomy.

If the learning outcome is to:	The test strategy could include:
Learn concepts	Cognitive learning, including knowledge (written test with multiple-choice, fill-in blanks, true/false questions), and comprehension (ask questions),
Interpret law, policy Apply knowledge to job tasks Reduce or prevent accidents	Cognitive learning, including analysis, synthesis, application Affective learning (examples, case study exercises, simulation)
Increase quality	Cognitive learning, including knowledge (checklist, drill) and application (role play)
Develop skills	Psychomotor learning (drill, practice, simulation)
Learn a process	Cognitive learning, including knowledge (checklist, written test with multiple-choice, fill-in blanks, true/false questions) and comprehension (ask questions),
Standardize, calibrate behavior	Psychomotor simulation with specific criteria and standards
Calibrate knowledge	Cognitive test items that reflect the levels of knowledge required

Table 10-2. Correlation of Test Strategies with Intended Learning Outcomes

Follow-Up Testing

Determine whether follow-up testing will be part of post-course evaluation. This might be appropriate as part of a large-scale training intervention or a professional development curriculum. Follow-up testing is done some period after the end of the course, for example after six months, to discover what the learner has retained and used. Results can help determine what needs to be added, deleted, or revised in the course.

Resources

If your test plan calls for electronic testing, then there are resources on the Internet that include freely downloadable scripts for multiple choice, true/false, and matching test items.

Some of them are:

Cut and Paste JavaScript web site:
http://www.infohiway.com/javascript/indexf.htm

Free CGI and Java scripts web site:
http://www.freebielist.com/scripts.htm

Script Search web site:

- Interactive surveys and voting:
  http://scriptsearch.internet.com/pages/l18c7c39.shtml

- Interactive Java tests and quizzes:
  http://scriptsearch.internet.com/pages/l18c7c41.shtml

- Interactive JavaScript tests and quizzes:
  http://scriptsearch.internet.com/pages/l4c7c41.shtml

- Interactive Perl tests and quizzes:
  http://scriptsearch.internet.com/pages/l9c7c41.shtml

Software for web-based tests and quizzes: http://www.ohj.com/

Please see the resource section at the end of this book for more URLs.

How to Forecast Training Tempests

Stormy training development weather is forecast by any of the test development symptoms below:

- Test items do not correlate to performance objectives.

- Learners complain that the test introduces new material.

- Learners with high test scores perform poorly on the job.

Step 5—Course Design

The design phase of the training project finalizes the method for accomplishing the project and prepares for content development. A design document is the outcome of this step.

A design document is a blueprint of the training course and details what the course will look like. It includes the purpose for the course, an overview of the learners, a list of prerequisites, objectives, course topics, content descriptions, a course outline, instructional methods, instructional media, descriptions of instructional activities, a description of evaluation methods, a course timetable that shows content sequencing with time requirements, and any required equipment or resources.

Final Review Prevents Costly Rework

The design document provides a final review of the course design before the time intensive task of content development begins. A review and sign-off on the design document by stakeholders—team leaders, customers, and subject matter experts—ensures that costly omissions, inappropriate focus, and errors in scope are avoided.

Training developers who feel rushed to show results in the form of content deliverables often overlook this step. Make the effort to perform this step. Refitting the design after content is developed is far more time consuming and costly than creating the design document.

Design documents can range in length from five to over 50 pages, depending upon the length and complexity of the project.

Project Plan and Design Document

The design document is different in purpose and focus from the project plan. The purpose of a project plan is to provide a business case for the project. Its focus is on resources needed for the training development project. The purpose of the design document, by contrast, is to detail the course design itself and to provide an opportunity to correct errors in the intended outcomes, as objectives and test criteria, and in the strategy prior to content development. Its focus is on the structure and content of the training course.

Components of a Design Document

The remainder of this chapter describes what a design document includes and what comprises each section.

Cover Sheet

The cover sheet includes a four or five line description of the purpose of the design document; the remainder is a sign-off sheet that includes the name of the author of the design document, the date it was prepared, the names of reviewers, and room for their signatures.

Table of Contents

A table of contents is included for longer documents.

Introduction

The introduction section includes:

Project name: This section provides the course title, its acronym, if any, and the release, version, or revision number of the course.

Project scope: This section describes the area covered by the project.

Project components: This section lists the deliverable components of the training solution, including printed and electronic materials.

Duration of course: This section estimates the amount of time learners will take to complete the course. Prepare this estimate with a caveat that it may be refined during the content development phase.

Class size: This section describes optimum, minimum, and maximum class sizes.

Prerequisites: This section describes any prerequisite courses, certifications, tests, or activities the learner must complete before attending the course.

Learners: This section provides a description of the target training population and includes: job titles, areas of responsibility, length of service with the company, background, previous and related experience, existing competencies, education level, attitudes, learning styles, media preferences, completed prerequisites, and course expectations. It should include any additional information that provides insight to the nature of the learner that would affect success in attaining the course goal.

Course goal: This section includes the course goal and describes the purpose of the training, how it fits into a curriculum (if applicable), and how the training will benefit the learner. The section includes the problems for which this training is a solution and includes the performance criteria that indicate successful achievement.

Course assessment and evaluation: This section is an overview of the methodology that will be used to determine the effectiveness of the training solution. It includes two components: feedback from the learners regarding the logistics of the training event and their perceived level of learning, as well as testing of the learners to determine their level of learning based on performance objectives.

Curriculum Roadmap

If the course is part of a curriculum, then this section identifies how this course fits into it.

Learner skills and knowledge: This section describes the prerequisite courses and activities in the curriculum that the learner must have completed before attending this course.

Certification requirements: This section describes what requirements this course satisfies in a curriculum that leads to certification.

Content Outline

Instructional resources: This section lists the course materials and the format in which they will be provided to learners, instructors, and administrators. This includes materials in printed or electronic form, and the prerequisite conditions for receiving the materials, such as network connections, or mail delivery.

Structure of material: This section describes each part that comprises the course, such as modules, chapters, lessons, and exercises. The description of each part includes what it contains, how long it takes, how it fits into the other parts, and its purpose. The following paragraph is an example of the description of a lesson:

A lesson contains an introduction, performance objectives, course content, a summary, and a learning assessment, such as a quiz or

review questions. A typical lesson takes one hour to complete.
Lessons that cover a common topic are grouped under a single
module.

Course and performance objectives: This section includes the
course objective and lists all performance objectives for the
course.

Instructional sequence and activities: This section lists the order
of course topics and a brief conceptual description of each. If there
is a consistent structural model on which each topic is based, then
it should be described here. For example, each chapter of a sales
solutions course might include market drivers, the technologies
that meet market needs, products that meet technology needs, and
sales opportunities for each product. Each chapter of a product
installation course might include customer problems that each
product solves, features and benefits of each product, installation
procedures for each product, and troubleshooting strategies for
selected products.

Content: This section is a description of each content segment,
including all structural levels, such as modules, chapters, lessons,
and exercises. The description is based on what the material
contains, rather than how it will be organized. If this is a product
course, the list of products covered in the course should be listed
here.

Delivery schedule: This section describes the anticipated time that
each content segment will take to complete during course delivery.
It can most conveniently and succinctly be expressed as a
timetable.

The following table is a generic example:

	Day 1	Hours	Day 2	Hours
AM	Lesson 1	1.0	Lesson 5	2.0
	Lesson 2	3.0	Application Exercise	2.0
PM	Lesson 3	2.0	Review	1.0
	Lesson 4	1.5	Certification Exam	3.0
	Review Exercise	0.5		

Table 11-1. Example of a Course Delivery Schedule

Development Requirements

This section includes the resources needed to develop the training product. They include: software, hardware, manuals, documentation, links, user identifications, security access, interfaces, programs, in-house personnel, consulting services, project team members, laboratory facilities, meeting facilities, testing equipment, tools, site tours, simulation equipment, video production equipment or crew, and any other materials and resources that are required for the facilitation and completion of the development process.

Delivery Requirements

This section includes resources required to deliver the training product. This can include many of the same items in the development requirements section.

Production Requirements

This section includes resources required to produce materials for the training product, such as network managers, media designers, video duplication services, printers, and any other resources that package the developed material into deliverable form.

How to Forecast Training Tempests

Stormy training development weather is forecast by any of the course design symptoms below:

- Stakeholders restrict you from using, or tell you to ignore, key analysis data.

- You are pressured to sacrifice interactive course activities because "they take too much time."

- You are pressured to add more topics, and alter the design to include more lecture.

- Stakeholders postpone signing-off on the design document.

- Stakeholders want to change the goal of the course, while still retaining the same development and delivery schedule.

Step 6—Content Development

You created a strong infrastructure prior to the content development step. You already know who the learners are, what they know, and what they need to know, as a result of your analyses. You have determined the goal of the course, the learning objectives, and how they will be tested. You have a roadmap—the design document—that includes topics to focus on, what order to address them in, and how long each will take the learner to complete. The design document also included a proposal of the instructional methods and media that seemed most appropriate to use. You are now well positioned to begin developing content.

Introduction to Media and Methods

This chapter introduces instructional media, instructional methods, and content that should be included in student and instructor guides. It is not intended to be comprehensive. It is intended to enable you to ask the right questions, so you can develop content that is appropriate for the level of your target learners' expertise, as well as for the design of your project.

Choose How to Implement the Design

All of the major design decisions have been made. In this step, you will finalize the choice of instructional methods and media, create content that links learning concepts, develop activities that implement learning concepts, and create materials that prepare the instructor while supporting the learner.

Like choosing upholstery for furniture, you have a variety of options for implementing the design. When choosing upholstery, your considerations include color, texture, durability, ease of cleaning, and other factors. Considerations for content development include physical appearance, usability, navigability, consistency, interactivity, relevance, application, pace, and matching the content level to learner expertise. This is the most creative step of the development process, and the most time-consuming one.

Levels of Expertise

Expert: Unknowingly aware, unconscious mastery

Experienced: Knowingly aware, knows what mastery requires, lacks mastery skills

Novice: Knowingly unaware, knows what basic competency requires, lacks basic competencies

Entry Level: Unknowingly unaware of what basic competency requires

---

Table 12-1. Levels of Learner Expertise

Levels of Expertise

In an earlier chapter, we examined levels of expertise and how that influences what can be learned. Your content needs to address the level of expertise at which the learners are at present, and to move them up one level at a time. Training that presents content above the learner's current level of expertise invites failure. Training that presents content at a level below the learner's expertise invites disinterest.

Be sure that the content and activities are consistent with the target learning population's level of expertise. Include a description of the target learning population's level of expertise in the instructor guide.

Shape Content for Adult Learners

Earlier we learned that adult learners want to:

* Begin learning from a point which is familiar to them, and then move to what is unfamiliar

* Solve realistic problems and address issues in their personal experience

* Avoid theory and history that do not directly relate to solving their problem

* Hear about what others are doing, and how those situations apply to the challenges they face

* Keep these guidelines in mind while developing course content and activities

Select Instructional Methods

Instructional methods are strategies for delivering content. I spent a lot of time deciding how to organize instructional methods for you—they can be described by many characteristics. I decided that since time, cost, and effort are driving factors in most training projects you will work on, the comparison table of instructional methods that follows is rated by time, cost and effort (complexity). I have also included factors that could influence your decision to select an instructional method (instructor expertise, degree of learner interaction, and the potential for enabling higher levels of learning).

What is Your Priority?	Lecture	Questions	Exercises	Discussion	Small Group Discussion	Facilitation	Guest Speaker	Panel of Experts	Brainstorming	Case Study	Role Play	Hands-On Experience
Development time	L	M	M	M	M	M	L	L	L	M	M	M
Cost	L	L	L	L	L	L	L M	L	L	L	L	M H
Complexity	L	L	L	L	L	M	L	L	L	L M	L M	M
Development time depends on instructor expertise	H	H	M	H	M	M	L	L	H	M	M	L
Degree of learner interaction	L	M	M H	M H	M H	H	L	L	L M	H	H	H
Potential for enabling higher levels of learning	L	M	M	M	M	H	L	L M	M	M	H	H

Legend
Requires a high (H), medium (M), or low (L) level of cost, time, or effort

Table 12-2. Course Development Characteristics of Instructional Methods

Lecture. In a traditional lecture method of instruction, the instructor speaks, the learners listen. The instructor's style determines whether questions are allowed. The lecture method of delivery offers limited or no opportunity for learner participation. This method can be appropriate for short presentations (one or two hours), information dumps, and squeezing a lot of information (that learners will not be expected to remember or master, but must be aware of) into a short period of time. It might also be appropriate where the learners have entry-level skills and knowledge, and are therefore limited in their ability to interact. Lecture-driven delivery can only be expected to yield lower levels of cognitive learning, such as basic comprehension and recall. In order to achieve higher cognitive levels of learning, the content can include drills, questions that require higher levels of cognitive activity, and exercises that cause learners to exercise higher levels of interaction and thought. The time, effort, and cost is rated as low, but could be rated as medium if the instructors have to be educated about the topic, or if the instructor material must be scripted rather than outlined.

Questions. Asking questions is an instructional method. Asking open questions, such as those that begin with who, what, when, where, and how, invite the learner to think rather than listen, and to interact rather than absorb. Questions should be strategically placed in the instructor guide to fuel interactivity. You might have noticed that I omitted *why* questions, which are also open questions. Over the years I have found that why questions invite confrontation more often than discussion. Asking *why* seems to force the learner into a defensive position, as if the questioner is challenging the learner's position. My advice is to use why questions sparingly—even in courses where introspection and attitude-change are the goals.

Exercises. Drills, quizzes, and simple individual or group games give the learners an opportunity to demonstrate knowledge and comprehension levels of cognitive knowledge.

Discussion. A structured discussion activity presents a multi-faceted topic to learners. Individuals or groups are assigned to defend different points of view. This method can cause learners to use application, analysis, synthesis, and evaluation levels of cognitive knowledge. The disadvantage is that most learners listen, and a handful of learners reap the interactive rewards of manipulating and expressing ideas.

Small Group Discussion. It has the same characteristics and advantages of discussion, with an additional advantage—more learners have an opportunity to participate. This instructional method has two levels: the small group discussion, where more or all learners have a chance to participate, and the report level, where a spokesperson presents the group's findings to the class.

Facilitation. This is an instructor-led process in which the instructor introduces a process, then coaches the learners through it by asking questions, introducing drills, providing or eliciting examples and job applications. It is a hybrid instructor-led method that is interactive and appropriate where learners have fundamental knowledge and skills to build upon, but not enough to be self-directed.

Guest Speaker. Transcribing the presentations of guest speakers is a low cost way of collecting course content. In order for it to be effective, you need to provide the speaker with a topic, learning objectives, time allocated for speaking, and questions that the presentation should answer. The level of learning that takes place using a guest speaker is parallel to the effect of a lecture, and can be elevated to higher cognitive levels of knowledge if the speaker's skills invite that kind of interaction with the learners. The advantage of a guest speaker is to present content about a specific topic on which most instructors are not fluent or which changes frequently, and would not be cost or time effective to continually update.

Panel of Experts. A panel of experts presents the same advantages of a guest speaker, and adds diversity. This method is appropriate where several points of view should be considered, or to provide a foundation for discussion or case study. You should prepare the panelists with a topic, the learning objectives, time allocated for the activity, and, if appropriate, a list of issues to address.

Brainstorming. This method is effective when learners are engaging in a change strategy. It is a problem-solving tool used to generate ideas. There is a facilitator who lists ideas that learners generate and asks open-ended questions that elicit application, analysis, synthesis, and evaluation level cognitive thinking.

Case Study. A case study is an activity that describes a real-life situation, or potentially real-life situation, poses a problem, asks for solutions, compares solutions with the real-life solution, and evaluates all solutions. Properly facilitated, this method can involve the higher levels of cognitive learning and affective learning.

Role Play. Role play requires the learner to act out a probable situation. It allows for coaching and immediate feedback in a supportive environment. Role play is most appropriate for practicing people skills, such as presentations, interviews, evaluations, and discussions, and can engage learning at the affective level (arousing feelings and emotions).

Hands-On Experience. This method simulates a real-life situation, using the tools and environmental cues that the learner will have access to or be required to use in a job situation. It is most appropriate for engaging learning at the psychomotor level (requiring physical action combined with thought).

Degrees of Realism

Most realistic

Simulation

Role play

Case study

Examples

Discussion

Least realistic

Table 12-3. Degrees of Realism. Realism Increases with the Use of Instructional Methods That Are Closer to Real-Life Situations

Your Experience Is a Resource

Think of the most effective learning experience you have ever had. What happened? How did it happen? What was it about the course design or what did the instructor do that made your experience possible? Ask others about their most memorable learning experiences. What works best in your industry?

Instructional Media

Media are the aids that implement the instructional methods. Following is an overview of the ones you are most likely to use. Most media applies to both classroom and electronic course delivery. How they are adapted for each is included in the overview.

Bound printed matter, usually in the form of books or binders, including instructor guides and student guides. They might also include resource manuals, such as glossaries, policies, procedures, guidelines, and other lengthy company documents. Bound printed matter is usually provided at the beginning of the course. They can be loaned or given as personal copies for each learner.

Handouts are short documents that are distributed when they are needed, such as exercises, assignments, and checklists. If there are many, and if nothing will be lost be providing them prior to when they are needed, then include them in the bound printed matter. This technique ensures that everyone will have a copy and saves handling and distribution time.

Overheads are paper-sized transparencies that can be run through a printer or photocopier like a piece of paper. Overheads can be used to provide an enlarged copy of what the learner sees in his material, or to illustrate a drawing, a flow of activities, or a hand-computation, projected onto a screen visible to the entire class. This media requires a transparency projector. Some organizations have transparency machines that use a roll of transparency film, which is scrolled over the viewing area. You can also overlay a transparency sheet over this type of projector.

Slides can be generated by camera or computer. They provide visual backup to instructor or text material. Camera-generated slides have to be manually inserted one at a time into a slide-holding carousel, fitted onto a slide projector, and shown linearly. They can be timed, but have no special effects or animation. Computer-generated slides can be changed or rearranged easily, have timing, animation, and special effects options, and can be hyperlinked with documents, spreadsheets, or any other kind of database, computer- or web-based file. Computer-based slide shows can be repurposed with notes for student guides, instructor guides, and web-based training. Special equipment is required to project a computer-based slide show.

Wall charts are most appropriate to use when a concept will be revisited, should be remembered, or provides a checklist. Use them to show learners where in the course you are, to chart milestones, or to make changes to an evolving situation. Determine whether they should be laminated to endure travel and repeated use, and what size they need to be. The font and images need to be easily visible from anywhere in a room. In a computer-based environment, this media effect can be accomplished by inserting a frame on a web page, which remains visible as the learner changes content pages.

Audio media includes tapes played with a tape recorder and streaming audio. Sounds on a computer course that provide course content should be accompanied by text, in case the learner does not have a sound card or speakers. An exception to this involves situations where the audio output is meant to test for sound discrimination in the learner. Audio is especially appropriate for material in which voice inflection, language skills, or sound recognition are crucial.

Video media includes tapes played in a video recorder and streaming video. Video should not be used as an integral part of content on a computer course unless all learners have access to bandwidth required for jitter-free playback. Video is appropriate for showing procedures, equipment, and behaviors that are difficult to describe.

Computer-based training (CBT) is a catchall phrase for training that occurs on a computer. It can be self-paced, programmed instruction, or a number of other formats. It is expensive, time-consuming, and complex to develop. Changes are expensive to make, and most CBT courses that I have developed and taken are little more than page-turners. The best CBT includes interactivity, lots of help, and easy navigation.

Distance learning is a term applied to training that takes place among geographically dispersed learners in real time. It includes traditional instructor-led methods that use telephone, satellite, radio, or broadband streaming technologies. A variety of technologies exist that enable the instructor to illustrate or add notations to a computer screen or communicate output from a whiteboard.

Web-based training includes print and multimedia delivery of course content. It does not include a live instructor or real-time interactions among learners. The course is constructed like a web site, and requires content design, site design, web site architecture design, and almost every other hardware and software consideration that a web site requires, including maintenance. It can be posted onto the Internet, an intranet, or a CD. One advantage of this media is that it is faster to produce: a slide show can be converted into HTML format, editing errors are easy to correct after posting, hyperlinks can easily be changed, and updates can be quickly added.

Content Flow and Priorities

Content should be organized based on the needs of the learner, e.g., by topics that build on one another; problems that range from easy to difficult; issues that are organized by frequency, urgency, or importance; or in whatever way supports the application of course content at the job.

Make content fit the purpose of the course, and the needs of the learners.

Content flow and priorities are indicated by analysis results and learning objectives. The point of bringing this up is to encourage you to think outside of the academic box most of us were raised in, which included irrelevant historical material, tangential developments, and other content that was not applicable or useful. Your guideline for content flow and priorities is to make content fit the purpose of the course, as well as the needs of the learners.

How to Structure Activities

Activities are learning events. An activity should include directions for the instructor, such as the purpose of the activity, time to allow for it, how to administer it, and suggested answers. Instructions should be incorporated for the learner that include the assignment and the time allowed for it.

Do not assume that if an instruction is included in the student guide that the instructor will notice it, or that if it is included in the instructor guide that the instructor will communicate it.

If an instruction is important for the successful timing or completion of the activity, then include it. Never assume that an instruction will automatically be understood to exist, or that the instructor will know the answers intended to be correct.

If there is no instructor, then include instructions with the assignment. Do not assume, for example, that a learner will know how to answer multiple-choice questions. Instruct them whether to choose one answer or more than one answer; whether to skip an answer they do not know or to mark their best guess, and how to indicate a correct answer (write it in or circle it, select it or deselect it).

What to Include in the Student Guide

Whether you call it a student guide, workbook, or learner manual, the first question to answer is whether to have one. Honestly, I cannot think of a situation where the learner would not benefit from having some form of documentation that includes:

- The goal of the course

- The learning objectives

- The key topics

- A roadmap of the course that estimates the time that each topic will take to complete

* The requirements for successful completion of the course

Additional necessary materials include a copy of assignments, tests, and key content, such as tables, illustrations, and new terms or acronyms.

In parts of the world where resources are scarce, learners must rely on their memories and their instructors for most of this information. The burden of helping them focus their direction falls squarely on the instructor. If you are developing a course under conditions where paper and computer resources are limited, then ensure that the instructor guide is complete and thorough.

Instructor-led course. A student guide for an instructor-led course should include the course goal, learning objectives, a roadmap, key concepts, exercises, requirements for the successful completion of the course, and all assignments. It can also include any visuals that the instructor will use, background articles, a bibliography, terms and acronyms, and any other material you think will be helpful, both during the course and afterward as a resource on the job.

Self-paced course. A self-paced course, whether in print or on the computer, should include the components named under the instructor-led course, plus information that an instructor would normally provide, such as background or preparation material, decision guides, self-tests, assignments, and answers to exercises, quizzes, or tests. Scoring that is immediately provided for computer-based tests can eliminate the need to provide test answers.

Computer-based course. A student guide for a computer-based course should include the components referred to in the instructor-led and self-paced courses. (Computer-based course does not refer to CBT, an instructional method, but to any course that is accessed through a computer.)

Include a document that describes how to find the course. It could be a printable document, separate and apart from the course, or a printed document, which includes directions to a geographical location, files to which to browse, or a URL. Outside the course, there should be directions on how to enter, navigate, and exit the course, as well as troubleshooting tips, and contacts for technical and content assistance. A guideline to what information should be included at a source outside of the course is whatever the learner will need to get unstuck if navigation or technical problems occur.

What to Include in the Instructor Guide

The instructor guide should include a copy of everything that is in the student guide. In addition, it should include answers to all activities that pose questions, such as exercises, quizzes, and tests. It should include background material that can help prepare the instructor, a rationale for the selection of instructional methods and activities, a schedule, a course map, resources, and directions for each activity. Include start time, end time, lunches and breaks on the schedule, as well as how long they should last. This helps instructors pace themselves.

Much of this content was developed for the design document, and can be inserted into the instructor guide with minor adjustments.

Layout of Instructor Guide

The design of an instructor guide is related to the level of expertise of your instructors. There is not a right, wrong, or best design.

If the instructor team does not include subject matter experts, include more background material and scripting in the instructor guide. You will need to include far more information than they will actually deliver, because instructors need to understand why and how things work, so that they can explain it.

An instructor guide for inexperienced instructors should include ample prompts. For example:

- Navigation guidance, such as *Tell the learners to turn to Page 76.*

- Questions to ask that invite interaction, such as, *Ask: Who can name two of the five types of programming languages?*

- Answers for any questions you write in the instructor guide.

- Guidelines for managing assignments, such as, *You have ten minutes to complete this assignment.*

Other Material

In addition to student and instructor guides, there are a number of materials that can enhance content delivery. They include:

Course media. Course media include any audio and visual materials that support the course content, such as tapes, movies, slides, overheads, wall charts, diskettes, CDs, and web sites. Each has its own production and maintenance requirements.

Audio or video production includes script writing, hiring talent, equipment scheduling, taping, editing, and final production. If you do not have time to learn or perform all of these tasks, consider outsourcing them.

Web site production includes site architecture designers, layout designers, content developers, a web master, and other talent that might need to be outsourced.

Job aids. Job aids are documents that include content that prompts the learner to remember important points while performing the job. It can include an illustration, flowchart, list, or checklist. It is

Design a job aid for the environment in which the learner will be using it.

used for reference, so it should be easy to read and serve as a reminder, not as a teaching tool. Design a job aid for the environment in which the learner will be using it. A credit card call center operator who sits in a low-walled cubicle will not have room to hang a poster, so design the job aid to fit the space they have. A professional driver, who repeatedly handles the same maps, could benefit from a laminated map, perhaps divided into sections that can be written on with erasable ink. Consider situations where a job aid would not be useful. A power line electrician uses both hands while working outdoors on a pole, and, for safety reasons, cannot handle items that could melt or burst into flames in the event of a flashover.

Usability Considerations for Course Materials

Factors to consider when designing course materials include:

- **Layout.** Layout considerations should include the experience level of the instructor, environmental constraints of the training event, and navigability.

- **Appearance.** Appearance considerations should include the distance from which the material will be seen, lighting conditions, and shapes or colors that add to the content message.

- **Reuse.** Reuse considerations should include whether the course will be delivered in more than one format, such as instructor-led and web-based.

- **Cost.** Cost considerations include durability of the materials, which depends on how they will be used (in outdoor weather conditions, repeatedly folded or rolled); varying formatting standards (videotape formats are different for North America and Europe); rental of equipment to support materials; adaptations for sites that require translation into another language; art, layout, printing, and other production costs; and revision of content.

- **Distribution.** The distribution of course content must take into account shipping, technical support, power requirements—including how many devices and outlets are needed, what equipment voltage requirements are, whether or not the equipment plugs will fit existing outlet configurations, and if power converters are required—and connection requirements for computers, such as secure Internet and intranet access.

- **Revision.** Revision considerations include whether to conduct courses that contain out of date material; and whether to update on an as-needed basis, including minor edits and content changes, or only at scheduled times, such as every six months.

Short List of Don'ts

There are a number of instructional techniques you should avoid including in your training course.

Do not have the instructor read out loud. Unless language recognition is part of the learning objective, reading out loud indicates a lack of preparation on the part of the instructor and demonstrates disrespect for the learners by treating them like elementary school children.

Do not have students read out loud. Unless reading out loud directly relates to a performance objective, it is inappropriate to have students read out loud. This practice creates a threatening learning environment for people with poor reading skills or for whom spoken English is difficult.

Do not spend time silently reading course material in class. Make required reading either a prerequisite to the course or a homework assignment. If the material needs to be covered, instruct the trainer to paraphrase the content. This method is not a productive use of expensive classroom time.

Minimize lecture. Lecture is fast, easy, and cheap to develop—and excludes the learner. Choose instructional methods that motivate learning by involving the learner.

How to Forecast Training Tempests

Stormy training development weather is forecast by the symptoms below, all of which complicate or extend the time, cost, or effort required to develop content:

- The content development phase is entered without a design document.

- Stakeholders have not signed off on the design document.

- The countries and languages in which course content will be used are undecided.

- You know nothing about the expertise level of the instructors.

- The course content mismatches the expertise level of target learners.

Step 7—Pilot and Verify

The first time the course is delivered in the classroom or is completed online is called a pilot. The pilot provides an opportunity to verify how well the course content, delivery logistics, facilities, materials, course design, and timeframes work. Feedback sources include class participants, observers, and the instructor(s).

The Goal

The reward that every instructional developer hopes for is to complete the pilot and receive comments that confirm that you achieved the course goal, verified the learning objectives, and confirmed the value of the course content. Ideally, the only changes you should need to make are minor modifications in timing, page numbering, typos, and transitions. You might discover that you need to reorder the flow of modules, or adjust the depth or time spent on a topic.

If the course was designed and developed according the systematic approach presented in this book, then those should be the extent of required changes—there should be no big surprises.

Whose Evaluation and Feedback Do You Want?

Obtain an evaluation of the course from each of the participants, observers, and the instructor(s). Participants can include members of the target population, subject matter experts, prospective instructors, and stakeholders. Include international members of the target population. Ask for feedback about ambiguous terminology, inappropriate terms, or activities that conflict with social customs.

The only observers in the pilot should be development team members. My personal bias is that anyone who does not participate in the process cannot provide valid feedback on how well it works—they can only provide feedback on how well it seemed to work, or how well others said it worked. I prefer first-hand feedback, and that is why I expect SMEs and stakeholders to attend the pilot as participants.

There are three kinds of feedback you want to have: participant course evaluations, instructor evaluations, and participant test results, which indicate performance.

Additionally, you will have comments and changes noted by the development team observer(s).

Computerized courses can provide an online evaluation form and test, and should be completed by a member of the development team prior to release.

How to Collect and Analyze Feedback

Ask questions that your development team feels are important to have answered. Use questions similar to those in the sample evaluation. The examples include questions that the learner can rate on a scale, as well as short-answer questions. Rated questions are easy to tally but are highly directive. Short-answer questions require more effort to sort and categorize, but invite learners to express honest feedback. A mix of both kinds of questions provides useful feedback.

Rated Evaluation Questions

On a scale of 1-10, with 10 being the highest or best score, please rate the following statements by circling your answer.

1. How valuable was this course in preparing you to <*insert course objectives*>? 1 2 3 4 5 6 7 8 9 10

2. How well was the course organized? 1 2 3 4 5 6 7 8 9 10

3. How clear were the learning objectives? 1 2 3 4 5 6 7 8 9 10

4. How effective were the case studies, examples, and other exercises? 1 2 3 4 5 6 7 8 9 10

5. How relevant was the course material to your situation? Please add comments in the feedback section below. 1 2 3 4 5 6 7 8 9 10

6. To what degree were you given opportunities to participate in your learning experience? 1 2 3 4 5 6 7 8 9 10

7. How useful was the student guide during class? 1 2 3 4 5 6 7 8 9 10

8. How useful do you think the student guide will be as a resource document on the job? 1 2 3 4 5 6 7 8 9 10

9. How knowledgeable was the instructor regarding course content? 1 2 3 4 5 6 7 8 9 10

10. How effective was the instructor in communicating the course content? 1 2 3 4 5 6 7 8 9 10

11. How effective was the instructor in dealing with learners? 1 2 3 4 5 6 7 8 9 10

12. How well did this course meet your personal needs? 1 2 3 4 5 6 7 8 9 10

13. How highly would you recommend this course to others? 1 2 3 4 5 6 7 8 9 10

Additional comments:

Table 13-1. An Evaluation Form with Questions That Are Rated from 1 to 10

Short Answer Evaluation Questions

- What did you like most about this course?
- What did you not like, or what seemed not to work well?
- What suggestions do you have for improving the learning experience?

Table 13-2. Evaluation Questions That Allow Unregulated Answers

Create a report that summarizes evaluative comments, participant performance results, instructor comments, and development team comments.

Include the averages of the numerically rated questions from the participant evaluation form, and note trends in feedback comments. Include only participants in the numerical tally.

Include non-participant ratings and comments, including yours, in a separate section of the summary. This separation provides clarity to the feedback, and will help you prioritize revisions.

Questions Verification Should Answer

The questions that a verification process should answer include:

- Does the course meet the learner's needs?
- Do the learners think that the course was of value?
- Do the materials support the learning objectives?
- Do the exercises work?
- Is the timing appropriate?
- Did the instructor have difficulty with the instructor guide, exercises, focus, or timing?
- Was the student guide an asset, a liability, or of no value?
- Did unsatisfactory comfort items complicate the learning environment (such as, room temperature, noise, lighting, breaks, and meals)?

Evaluation and Feedback

An evaluation appraises worth or value. Feedback communicates ideas to develop or changes to make. Erroneously, the terms are often used interchangeably. The end of course evaluation is commonly known as a smile sheet—meaning that it offers little value as a feedback tool. You can remedy this by recognizing the difference between evaluation and feedback, and designing your end of course evaluation so that it asks for feedback as well. It does not matter what you call the form, as long as you collect qualitative responses, as well as quantitative responses.

Include 15 minutes at the end of the course to complete the evaluation and feedback form. Include instructions for the instructor to administer the process, so that is not rushed, and so the learners have time to complete it thoughtfully. For online courses, ensure that the end of a unit or course has a link to the feedback page. Make the feedback process easy, and you will be more likely to have ongoing feedback that has value.

Wordsmithing Invites Valuable Comments

Take the time to consider what feedback you want to collect. Ask for what you want to know. This might seem fundamental, but many evaluation instruments are carelessly worded, or worded in such a way that the respondent feels trapped, having no outlet for suggestions or complaints.

This table provides an example of what you want to know, how to ask for it, and how not to ask for it.

What you want to know	Questions to ask
	Questions to avoid
Was the instructor an asset to the learning process and in what ways?	How knowledgeable was the instructor regarding course content? How effectively did the instructor: • Communicate course content? • Administer exercises? • Handle questions, concerns?
	How knowledgeable was the instructor? *How would you rate the instructor?*

Table 13-3. Examples of Poorly Worded and Well-Worded Evaluative Questions

How to Forecast Training Tempests

Stormy training development weather is forecast by the symptoms below:

• Comments you hear from course participants is very different from feedback results.

• Instructors complain that the course is difficult to deliver.

• Participants leave the room for extended periods.

• No online feedback is submitted.

• A small percentage of course registrants complete the online course.

Step 8—Evaluate and Revise

Revision is the process of correcting errors such as page numbering and spelling, adjusting timing or sequence, modulating processes such as exercises, test questions, and examples, updating or changing content, such as product features or company priorities, and adding or deleting content, such as products, which have been added or taken out of service.

First Revision

The revision stage of a new course follows the pilot and is based on evaluative comments from the instructor, target learners, subject matter experts, stakeholders, and the development team.

If you were loyal to the instructional design process, then the initial revision should include revelations but no surprises, and adjustments but no major reworking of the design or content.

Allow one to two days of revision for each day of training. Add time for SME review, editing, and printing. Uploading to an existing, debugged web site can be done daily as changes are completed.

Subsequent Revisions

Change is inevitable in business, and training needs to be current. Review and revision of courses should be an ongoing process.

How often you revise depends on the training environment of the course content. You may need to revise a course every two months in a high technology environment, every six months in a sales environment, and every two years in a virtually unchanging environment.

Sometimes unscheduled revision is required. Events that can precipitate course revision include changes in corporate focus, business climate, and technology. Following are examples of each type of change.

Corporate focus. A start-up training consulting firm that I worked with on the East Coast established itself by selling to any organization that would purchase more than 25 units of its single product. By the time the consultancy's earnings topped $15 million, the core product was diversified to meet the needs of six major markets. The company developed satellite courses, which supported the core course, and a consulting intervention that wrapped around the training courses. The collection of products became an organization change intervention, and individual products retained their integrity as stand-alone sales solutions. Revisions inserted market-specific examples to the core course for each new market. The revision retained the original course instructional and layout design. Only the examples changed.

Internal training needs also changed at this company. For example, a change in sales objectives created a need for a different focus in sales training. Small companies were no longer of interest to this growing consultancy. The new focus became major market accounts with assets of over $500 million. Sales goals for account managers were elevated from $300,000 to almost $1,000,000 per year. There was a turnover of sales representatives caused by the evolution in competencies they needed to demonstrate—a change from selling training classes to small accounts to collaboratively selling organizational change interventions to large enterprises. Sales training was revised to reflect the changes in business direction and the competencies of the target population.

Business climate. When I worked for AT&T in the 1970s, it was a monopoly. The turbulent business climate, during deregulation of the industry in the 1980s, created a need for expansive changes in the way business was done. Changes that affected training content during this period of downsizing and growth included new skill sets in the employee population, additional legal requirements, changes in telephony installation stimulated by requirements for access to central offices by third party companies, and new technological developments.

Technology. As a contractor for a leading internetworking company experiencing explosive growth, I was part of a team of training developers that revised the content of several product-dependent courses targeted for sales representatives and systems engineers. For each 1800-page course, there were several minor revisions, and two major revisions in one year. Changes included adding new product features, deleting products whose life cycles had ended, and adding new products. The company's sales approach and market focus changed at least three times, which meant updating examples, case studies, and content for student and instructor guides. We created intranet and CD versions of the instructor-led printed version. Revision was a full-time job, and required a course maintenance team.

Managing the Revision Process

Correcting editing errors and making low priority updates will always be required. It is a good idea to establish a revision process for two reasons:

- If you have determined a routine for making revisions, then they are more likely to be done on a regular basis, thereby keeping the course current.

- An established process avoids the temptation to correct minor editing errors as they are found, and discourages impulsive rewrites, both of which can be unnecessarily time-consuming.

There are several steps to effectively managing a revision process:

- **Establish the frequency of the process.** Determine a cycle for revision, e.g., monthly, quarterly, or yearly. The cycle should reflect the needs of the business. For example, it does not make sense to establish a yearly revision process for a fast-growing software company whose product revision cycle is two months.

- **Establish the extent of the process.** Determine whether you need two categories of revisions: major and minor. Major revisions are done less frequently than minor revisions and can include course redesign, extensive content reorganization or update, changes in objectives, course-wide changes in formatting or editing, and changes that address a changed training population. Minor revisions include a few edits, page renumbering, and minor updates in content. Minor revisions are scheduled more frequently than major revisions. If you decide to have only one category of revisions, all revisions will be done at each scheduled revision.

- **Announce the process.** Let people know what the revision cycle is. Educate them about the kind of changes that are normally made during each revision. Set their expectations so that you can manage time spent on the revision process, but be flexible enough to accommodate a truly pressing need for timely updates that do not fit the revision schedule.

- **Request changes.** Ask learners, SMEs, and other stakeholders to submit changes as they find them. Make this easy for them to do by accepting voice-mail and e-mail notifications. Provide an update form in the instructor and student guides— make it simple.

Ooops! Found an Error
Course 725: Lumber Mill Equipment Maintenance

Please describe the error and the page number or URL on which you found it:

We might have questions. How can we reach you?
Name:

E-mail: Phone:

< *Note to development team: Include the mail, fax, phone, and e-mail addresses to which updates should be sent.* >

Table 14-1. Example of an Error Report Form

- **Keep a file of update notices.** Organize a way to retrieve updates you receive from participants, SMEs, stakeholders, and development team members.

- **Respond to suggestions graciously.** Thank respondents and inform them of the next scheduled revision date. It is a good idea not to commit to making all suggested changes. You may find that you receive conflicting suggestions (from instructors), or that revisions in one module may negate the need for change in another.

Consistency of Style over Time

Courses revised by different team members over time with different writing styles, different ideas about what is important, and allegiances to different style guides can cause revision to take more time that necessary. Create a style guideline that provides a consistent voice and format. It should include writing and illustration guidelines.

Numbering Conventions

The most important reason to have a numbering convention for your training course is for easy reference to pages, and to differentiate versions of the course.

Numbering conventions should reflect the nature of your business and the way the content is used. For example, most courses will only require a course number, version number, and a consistent page numbering system.

A newly introduced course, which has been piloted and revised (debugged), is typically numbered 1.0.

Major revisions are indicated with whole numbers, such as, 1.0, 2.0, and 3.0. Minor revisions are indicated by decimal numbers, such as, 1.1, 1.2, and 1.3. For example Course 725, Version 2.3, represents version 2 (the first major revision after the original course, which is always Version 1), third minor revision.

Content that must be easy to reference by number, for example, by headings, should have numbers that precede the text title. A complex system could include a course number, version number, chapter number, and heading number. For example, the sixth heading of Chapter 10 in the second version, third revision of Course 725 would be referred to as 725.23.10.6. Within the course, units would include only the chapter and heading number, for example, 10.6 or 10.06.

Keep the numbering system as simple as possible. Training rarely requires an oppressive numbering system. Include the date of revision in the front matter, and the version in the front matter and bottom of either odd or even pages.

© 1997-2001, The Learning Edge   IDTW v2.1—10.6

Table 14-2. Example of How to Number Course Pages

The footer example above includes copyright information, the course acronym (IDTW), course version (2.1), chapter number, and page number (Chapter 10, Page 6).

How to Forecast Training Tempests

Stormy training development weather is forecast by the evaluation and revision symptoms below:

- Stakeholders resist budgeting for ongoing revision.

- The error reporting system does not work—you are not receiving reports of errors from instructors.

- Evaluations are not getting to you in a timely fashion.

- Evaluations are being reviewed and discussed by subject matter experts, instructors, and other stakeholders—with you excluded from the review loop.

The Finished Product

Congratulations. You have developed an effective training course. Here are some tips that will help you survive your success.

Smile When They Call Your Baby Ugly

Developing a training course requires you to create something from nothing, similar to a gestation and birthing process. You will receive feedback about the course that might not always be complimentary, and it is easy to take it personally. Receive feedback graciously. Here are some responses for dealing with comments that people make.

- *Thank you.*
- *I'll make note of it.*
- *Thanks for taking the time to let us know about that.*

- *What do you suggest?*
- *Tell me more about your ideas.*

It is not appropriate to be defensive. Few of the folks who give you feedback will realize you were the developer. If you assume that their intention is to be helpful, it is easier to depersonalize the feelings you might have and focus on the content improvements they suggest. Comments that indicate you are personalizing feedback include:

- *Whadd'ya mean?*
- *I don't agree with you.*
- *I talked with* <insert one or two impressive SME's names here> *and this is what they said is right.*

Completing Your Journey

Course development is a long, sometimes difficult journey. If you are prepared, do the right things, and convince your stakeholders to let you follow this systematic process, then it can also be efficient, cost-effective, and personally rewarding. I wish you success.

What's Next

The next section includes chapters that advise you how to manage training projects and customize training courses.

Section 3:
Manage and Customize

Managing the Training
Development Process

Any training development process needs to be managed. Whether you are a full-time project manager, or the one person to whom all of the project responsibilities are channeled, there are several points you need to remember to keep your training project moving toward a successful conclusion.

Identify Stakeholders

Identify who your stakeholders are and discuss the project with all of them. Stakeholders are people who have the power to direct, change, impede, and facilitate the success of your project. They can include funding resources, internal customers, parties affected by the training project, subject matter experts, and trainers.

Whether you meet face-to-face, or have discussions by way of e-mail, include everyone in every communication that defines the boundaries, scope, and definition of the project. A stakeholder who was not included in the initial discussion and who did not agree to the terms of the project can derail your timeline and budget. Make the identification of stakeholders your first priority when discussing a new training project.

A stakeholder who was not involved in the initial discussion can derail your timeline and budget.

Inform and Confirm

Stakeholders often send a representative to meetings. If this happens, then consider any agreements or opinions that you receive from a representative as non-binding, despite assurances that the representative is speaking for the stakeholder. Ensure that the stakeholders are updated about commitments made on their behalf, and confirm their agreement before moving forward. Do not rely on second-hand agreements.

Clarify Expectations, Desired Outcomes

Clarify expectations and desired outcomes from each stakeholder. You will likely collect expectations and desired outcomes that differ, and that might conflict. Identifying and resolving these will help to clarify your task and set priorities. Following are example questions, some answers you might receive, and what action you need to take:

- **What do you expect the training to look like?** The ideal answer is a consensus that says the decision is totally up to you. It is more likely that stakeholders will have some format in mind. For example, one person might envision a five-day instructor-led course, another a 15-hour online course, and yet another a training event that can be delivered internationally in six months. These expectations require dramatically different approaches, design, budgets, and development time. Resolve this by directing your questions to probing what problem needs to be solved, whether training is the answer, who the learners are, and if there is a time or budget constraint.

- **What behavior, results, or other differences do you expect the training to achieve?** For example, that the call center complaint rate will drop 25 percent, that sales revenues for Product X will double, that systems engineers will be able to design network solutions using the company's products, or that software development time will be reduced by 60 days. Do not accept these standards of measurement unless you know how to achieve them. Ask the stakeholder to tell you more about that very interesting statistic and how it was derived. The solution that brings about changes as specific as the examples above might require more than training. Organizational change and support might also be a part of the solution.

Manage Expectations, Offer Options

Some expectations and desired outcomes are unrealistic. Responsible project managers inquire about the rationale for such expectations and outcomes. This is a normal and expected part of the pre-planning phase. Ask questions such as: How did you determine that number? Why is that specific percentage your goal?

Find out what items are non-negotiable—delivery date, development team size, scope of the project, initial (pilot-phase) deliverables. Manage negotiable items to create the most successful training project outcome possible.

Set realistic expectations by offering options. Imagine that you have been asked to develop a 30-hour multimedia course to be distributed nationally in three weeks. This is an unrealistically short timeframe for a multimedia course. You will need to educate stakeholders about the time, cost, and personnel requirements for such a project, and then offer them options.

Options you *can* offer, for example, include one two-hour multimedia chapter or an instructor-led course delivered by the target date, or alternatively, a multimedia course deliverable one year from now. Options enable stakeholders to decide what their opportunities and priorities are.

Discuss Deliverables

Discuss the deliverables that stakeholders expect to receive, when they can expect to receive them, and in what form (final or draft, printed or electronic). During many of my new-project meetings, stakeholders have specified tangible items—such as a compact disc or a workbook—that they want the learner to have before the goal of the project has even been defined. Such decisions are premature, but you need to be aware of expectations about deliverables. Find out the story behind the request. A tangible product can be like a talisman to the stakeholder, who can show it to others, talk about it, and offer to let people see it. It has value and demonstrates results. If the stakeholder's request is consistent with the success of the course, then it is a good business practice to do what you can to provide the requested deliverables.

The story that follows illustrates the point. A sales manager at a large chemical company told me that he needed a computer-based training program. He specified that he must be able to demonstrate the course using a laptop computer. He felt that this would prove to his boss that he had the technical

Deliverables are not the project. They are a component of the project. The form they take is determined by the goals of the training.

expertise to qualify for a promotion to a newly formed position—Director of Information Systems. There was no relationship, of course, between the instructional media of the course and his professional qualifications. He seemed to think that an association with the project would give him the technical credibility he needed. What he requested turned out to be consistent with what would work best for the training audience. Financial and time budgets supported development of a computer-based course. He was able to introduce it to his boss with a laptop computer demonstration. He was promoted to the position he wanted—he had convinced others that he knew more about computers than anyone else at the company.

Do the best you can to find out why a particular deliverable is important to your stakeholders.

Tactfully educate stakeholders about the development process, and in what way appropriate deliverables facilitate the success of the course. Acknowledge and appreciate their suggestions; take their suggestions under advisement until you can determine what deliverables best fit the course.

Specify What Is Not Included

Ask your stakeholders to be specific about content that the training project should *exclude*. This could be a product nearing the end of its life cycle, a set of tasks that the target audience performs that has no bearing on training goals, or job-related examples from a region using atypical procedures.

If information collected in the analysis step indicates that products, procedures, or topics that stakeholders have requested should be excluded, then inform the stakeholders, include your findings in the analysis report and design document, and obtain their sign-off on recommended exclusions before implementing the exclusions.

Follow Project and Design Plans

The project plan and the design document provide focus and direction. While they are subject to corrections and revisions, be sure to manage the project according to plan. If a problem develops, it is easier to take corrective action if differences can be correlated between where you are and where you *should* be.

Use Planning Tools

Planning tools help you coordinate and monitor time, cost, and resources. Software planning tools will save you steps in a complex project because they perform several steps concurrently. You can develop and edit timetables, assignments, and costs with

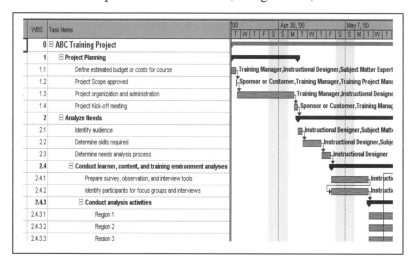

Table 16-1. Excerpt from a Project Planning Tool

minimal effort. A spreadsheet program might fit your needs if your team is small, if the timeline short, or if your activities, content, and deliverables are minimal.

Monitor Non-Negotiable Deadlines

Closely monitor the time and monetary budgets you have set. If you have a non-negotiable delivery deadline, then consider what can be omitted, postponed, or delivered in draft form if your timeline slips.

Time-estimating provides a guideline for anticipating each step in the training project. The skills of team members, the responsiveness of subject matter experts, and any changing conditions contribute to the accuracy of your estimates.

Collaborate

Collaborate with other departments to reduce redundancy and avoid costs. Collaborative discussions facilitate multipurposing your training material. Find and use what exists. Tell others what you are doing. At the beginning of your project, publicize your training goal in an internal newsletter or intranet news area—describe your focus, the benefits to the learners, and how the project supports the corporate goal. These techniques invite others to tell you about similar programs.

How to Forecast Training Tempests

Stormy conditions for project management are forecast by the following conditions:

- Stakeholders discourage or try to reduce the time you have budgeted for analysis, or pressure you to cut your development time estimates in half.

- Subject matter experts do not return material they are supposed to review or edit by your drop-dead deadline.

- Training-delivery technology is driving your development decisions.

- Bottlenecks in resources or time are not reported to you.

Customizing Off-the-Shelf Courses

Development time can be drastically reduced if an existing course, or modules from a course, can be adapted to your use. Existing courses that are available for purchase are called *ready-made* or *off-the-shelf* courses. Internal courses provide a resource that can be adapted for your target learning population.

Searching for an existing course with a good fit to your training need is like buying a ready-to-wear suit. You can get the size, style and color you want, but might have to alter the sleeves, leg cuffs, or waistband. An off-the-shelf course can be close to what you want, but might require customization.

Must you customize? Certainly not. But as with a suit with the sleeves an inch too long, a poor fit creates a poor impression, and never feels right. Course content that the learner considers credible, relevant to the job, and useable has the best fit and fosters behavior change.

How to Find Off-the-Shelf Courses

Determine what you want. Some people shop for off-the-shelf courses the way they shop for casual clothes—instead of first determining what they want, then looking for it, they trust that they will recognize the *right* one when they see it. Selecting an off-the-shelf course should be done with the care given to buying an expensive suit—with a clear idea of where it will be worn.

Before selecting an off-the-shelf course, determine the course goal, who the learners are, and what they need. This means developing a preliminary project plan, conducting analyses, and drafting objectives. Then you will know what needs the course must satisfy.

Evaluate products before finalizing your course design. The search for off-the-shelf material can begin as soon as you know the course goal. Gather facts and invite vendors to talk with you early in the development process. However, be aware that an evaluation of the material will be valid only after you know what the course requires. Evaluation can precede, or be concurrent with, finalizing the course design.

Determine time and budget allocations. Gain agreement with your stakeholders about time and budget allocations for the search and evaluation of off-the-shelf courses. Sometimes they will want to include everything in your existing budget, and sometimes they will allocate additional money and time for those tasks. The latter is more desirable if you are exploring the possibility of using an off-the-shelf program but have no recommended candidates.

Determine who the vendors are. Ask colleagues for recommendations. Go to your professional organizations, other departments of your company, Internet news lists, and mailing lists related to your topic, professional magazines, and consulting companies. Use the search feature on your Internet browser to look for products that might suit your needs.

Interview vendors and pilot their products. Make a list of prospective vendors. Interview them, listen to their presentations, and review their course material. Have the top two or three vendors present the course for evaluation to you and an audience of the intended target population. You might have to pay for the instructor's travel and living expenses, as well as a course delivery fee, the latter of which should be applied to your purchase.

If you are interested in an online course, then visit web sites that offer online courses by a variety of corporate and individual authors. Course advertisements include course descriptions, usually written by the vendor, and some offer content previews. Take time to inspect the course outline and objectives. Read participant reviews and take time to step through the preview if there is one.

Many online courses are submitted to training resource sites by amateurs who use the sites as self-publishing venues, so make sure that your team members thoroughly review the material themselves.

What to do if no off-the-shelf products fit your need. If you discover that none of the vendors have appropriate material for you to work with, then continue your project development by roughing out the criterion test items and completing the instructional design document. You have already done a preliminary project plan, analyses, and objectives. You can then begin content development.

If you find an off-the-shelf product that will complete part of your course development requirement, then adopt it and adjust the project plan accordingly. The final design document should describe what material will be covered by off-the-shelf material, how it needs to be customized, and what needs to be developed.

How to Assess Off-the-Shelf Courses

An off-the-shelf course should meet your training needs. Guidelines are included in the table below.

✓	The course goal matches your training outcome.
✓	The course objectives support the course goal and your training outcomes.
✓	The lesson objectives are behavioral, measurable, and support the course objectives.
✓	The content matches the focus that your learners need.
✓	The vendor provides an option for you to customize the course.
✓	The vendor provides trainer training, or is willing to learn about your business by meeting your learners and working with you to add learner-specific examples.
✓	The course can be delivered to your specifications in the time required.

Table 17-1. Checklist for Assessing Off-the-Shelf Courses

A missing check mark from any of the items in the checklist would be a deal-killer for me. That is because the items in the checklist are critical foundation items. If they are missing, then you might as well build the course yourself rather than lose time making major alterations to a poor fit.

On the other hand, if an existing course matches your training outcome, and is missing one goal of several, then it can provide value to your training project. Just add and integrate the missing components.

The key to sound course selection is to carefully screen for the one that most closely fits what you would develop yourself; that is, one that matches the project plan and design document.

How to Customize Courses

Focus. If the course you want to develop requires an industry-specific focus, then the most reasonable place to look for an off-the-shelf one is within the industry. If you find an industry-specific course, then your customization efforts will be streamlined—focusing on developing company examples, practices, and procedures.

If the course you want to develop is a job-specific course that is done across many industries, then the most reasonable way to search for an existing one is by job or organization title. Examples of job titles that cross industry boundaries include network engineer, accountant, EEO coordinator, and administrative assistant. Examples of organizations or functions that are common to all industries include human resources, accounting, and information technology. Your customization efforts for this kind of course would focus on developing examples within your industry and company.

Content. The content of a course is most credible when it uses professional and industry terms correctly, when examples represent common, frequent, or likely events, and when job application exercises are recognizable as events that could actually happen during a work cycle.

Examples. If you are not a subject matter expert, and few instructional designers and developers are, then be sure to carefully record incidents shared with you during interviews in the analysis step of the instructional design process. Incidents that people describe in the analysis phase often provide material for real-life examples and applications. Look for answers to questions such as:

- What was difficult to learn?

- What do you wish you had known before starting the job or task?

- What would you recommend that others do?

Subject matter experts. Consult with subject matter experts to fill in any gaps in the stories you collected that might be material for examples, case studies, exercises, and test questions. I specifically recommend that you consult with more than one expert. Doing this will help you to determine which practices are normal and which are stylistic.

What to exclude. Examples that you collect of anomalous behavior or bizarre situations can be impressive, but hard for the learner to apply to the every day work environment. Use examples of situations that commonly occur or are costly to be unaware of—regarding safety, expense, and time.

Customize from the top level down. Customize a generic course from the top level down to the bottom level. Start with the course goal, and work down through the course objectives, to the lesson objectives, and then to the lesson content. This top down approach ensures that there will be a consistent fit for your target audience throughout the generic course.

When customizing a generic course, work from the top level down. This top down approach ensures that there will be a consistent fit for your target audience.

Symptoms of a poor fit begin at the top level. If the course goal is a close fit, but not on target, then my suggestion is to not use the course. Drop it and focus your efforts on finding or developing a course that will work for your learners. You will spend as many hours trying to make the wrong course fit as you would developing it yourself. A course that learners recognize as tailored for them—that fits their needs—will be far more successful than one that is close, but not on target.

Resources

Peer referrals. Ask for referrals from other professionals in your field—some of your colleagues have already done the footwork you are about to do. Ask who provides the best service and who has the best products for the learning outcome you must satisfy. Try not to limit yourself to your immediate circle of friends and acquaintances. Log onto chat rooms and lists that serve your profession.

Professional organizations. Contact professional organizations and ask for ten companies that offer off-the-shelf training in the field or on the topic in which you are interested.

Peer referrals and professional organizations that serve your target training population will know the most about what you want when you describe your needs. However, there are additional resources you should be aware of.

If you cannot find referrals for vendors within your field, then ask for resources from the American Society for Training and Development (ASTD) and the International Society for Performance Improvement (ISPI).

ASTD (http://www.astd.org) focuses on the needs of training professionals and provides extensive resources to support that focus. It serves over 70,000 members in 100 countries. The organization offers a catalogue of training-related books, a buyer's guide of training products with over 400 topics, and software that facilitates training administration and delivery.

Be sure to shop around before buying the ASTD brand or ASTD-endorsed software. Prices range between $400 and $700, and much of the interactive testing and gaming software is downloadable as freeware. (See the chapter on ready-made scripts for online training components that you can download free.)

ISPI (http://www.ispi.org) is a much smaller organization than ASTD, with a membership of 10,000 in 42 countries. It focuses on performance improvement, which includes training as one component. Its stated mission is to improve productivity and performance in the workplace.

A search of the Internet will provide resources that fit most of your needs. However, you might feel overwhelmed by the number of options. Be prepared to sift through a lot of amateurish material. There is also material written by people who are knowledgeable about your topic, or who are talented multimedia designers, but whose products are not instructionally sound.

Internet keyword search. A search using the phrase *training course suppliers* returned a list of many thousands of web sites. A more selective search is likely to provide resources that you can follow up with in your field.

Convention listings and marketplaces. The following web sites include examples of convention, trade show, and seminar listing sites, as well as marketplaces where training vendors pay to have their products and services listed in a centralized, searchable format.

- America's Learning Exchange consortium (ALX) is a training supplier marketplace supported by the U.S. Department of Labor and a number of corporate partners. It links to thousands of training products and vendors. Its stated mission is to provide public information about, and access to, educational and training resources, as well as to provide a marketplace for those resources. http://www.alx.org

- Prometheon Learning Resource Network is a marketplace site, which includes scheduled public training courses, courses for purchase, a speakers bureau, a library, and links to training resources. The site is searchable by topic, course name, and city. http://prometheon.com

- Trade Show Central includes listings for over 50,000 trade shows and 30,000 seminars and conferences. Although its underlying purpose is to sell services to event exhibitors, it also includes a large database of events and suppliers. You can search the site by any keyword you wish. There are lists of categories to choose from. All of the high technology topics are grouped under Information Technology. The benefit of this site to you is that this is a way to find out names of companies that offer courses on topics in which you are interested. If your training population is small, then you might opt to send trainees to general public seminars. If your training population is large, then you can inquire if the company is willing to customize their generic program to fit your needs. http://ww2.tscentral.com

If you discover a web site that you think is a valuable resource for off-the-shelf courses, please send me an e-mail with the URL and

I'll post it on my web site so that others can benefit from your discovery.

Address your e-mail to me at riveshc@lepublishing.com.

University programs. Colleges, universities, and trade schools offer certificate programs in specialized fields. They sometimes contract with outside vendors or leaders in their fields to deliver courses. These instructors can be a resource for you or might provide leads to still other resources.

Directories. Training directories are available on hundreds of topics. A search on Amazon.com for *training directories* listed titles in a wide variety of industries.

Online Courses

There are thousands of online courses for sale, available on disc, or by subscription. The market is easy to enter, and there are thousands of poorly designed and developed courses mixed into thousands of well-designed and well-developed ones. If you do not have a recommendation from a source you trust to help you narrow down the list, you can lose a lot of time sifting through them; use online course reviewers to help speed this task along.

Online course reviewers usually have an underlying business goal of selling you something, which could be existing products or consulting services. But if they list the kind of training courses you need, then their reviews can save you time. Here are some examples of online course reviewers:

- Click2Learn sells e-learning products, services, and resources that help companies develop, deliver, and manage online training. The *How-To Center* page lists online courses for purchase, and provides reviews of them through Lguide: http://www.click2learn.com

- Lguide reviews of hundreds of professional, personal, and academic online courses. Each topic includes a brief description of compared courses summarizing the intended audience and their skill level, the publisher, the price, the course duration, an evaluation, and the pros and cons of the

204   Developing Training Courses ▶ **Manage and Customize**

course. Detail for each course includes a course description and an evaluation of the content, design, delivery, and overall value. If you need additional help, Lguide also offers consulting services that help you decide which course is right for you. As we go to print, they announced they would become a subscription site, but would allow a free review period of 30 days. http://www.lguide.com

- Headlight.com provides e-learning solutions and offers a long list of business courses, many for IT professionals. It offers over 3,000 courses, which include categories for web development, business, IT certification, desktop, and IT professionals. Each category includes a list of course titles, a two-line description, and the publisher. Next to each course title is listed the minimum required modem speed, the skill level of the course, its duration, and its price. Each title includes links to course detail and the publisher. The course detail includes an overview, a syllabus, technical requirements, and a form that users can complete to review the course. The publisher link opens to an overview of the company and a link to its web site. http://www.headlight.com

- The Training Registry links to a variety of training resources. It lists training courses, providers, products, and facilities. Course descriptions are only two lines in length, but provide links to the provider's web site. The strength of this site seems to be that training providers can be located by country (Canada, the United States, Australia, and United Kingdom); by province or state; by city; or alphabetically by name. This provides a convenient way to find out who is listed in your area, but bear in mind that, as a registry, it includes only those organizations that have signed up with it. http://www.trainingregistry.com

Writing for International Markets

The company for whom you develop training might be regional, national, international, or foreign. The company's customers might have a different demographic profile from the people who staff the company. Its employees might be culturally and linguistically diverse. How can you develop training courses that will be appropriate, understandable, and useful to culturally different audiences?

This chapter describes questions that you should ask during the development process, and provides guidelines for designing internationally considerate content.

Globalize or Localize?

Globalize means to create training content and materials that are readable and useable anywhere in the world: the same course is simply translated into different languages.

Courses that teach a specific methodology or that are primarily informational are candidates for globalization.

Localize means to customize training content and materials for a country or a specialized group. Localizing training materials require different examples in course content, different instructional methods—including changes in the instructor guide—and changes in administrative guidelines.

Candidates for localization are courses that require behavior change and human interaction.

Questions to Ask

Questions that you need to ask include:

- How fluent is the target audience in the language in which I am writing the course? Consider written and spoken fluency.

- Should translators be included on the development team?

- Should translators have content knowledge? How fluent do they need to be in the technical terminology and concepts of the course?

- Will you need multilingual instructors and materials? Will translators be required in the class during delivery?

- How much time, personnel, and cost need to be added for each version or translation of the course?

- What conventions should be included in the course materials to express distance, date, temperature, time, speed, and other international differences?

- In what languages are training materials legally required to be? For example, if you are developing a course for use in Canada, the course must be available in English and French.

Translation Dilemma

Internal training should be applicable and useful to all employees. Customer training needs to be accessible and understandable to all markets that purchase your company's products. Ideally, training should be delivered in the native language of the training population. If internal training is delivered to German nationals who speak German during the course of their jobs, then the training delivery and training materials should be in German—even if the training does not take place in Germany.

If training must be delivered in a language that is not native for groups in the training population, then find out about their fluency in the analysis step. Do they have better reading or speaking skills? If their speaking skills are better, consider minimizing or eliminating reading material. If their reading skills are better, consider a self-paced course, or course activities that include same-language group work.

If you cannot find instructors who have multilingual skills, consider including translators during each course delivery. Your development time should include orientation of the translators to course content, concepts, and terminology.

Special Needs Learners

Your target audience might include learners with special needs. For example, will multilingual sign language professionals be required?

How to Write Clearly for International Audiences

Sometimes technical communicators hurry through a sentence, trying to cut out words that seem trivial, such as modifiers, adjectives, and verbs, or use jargon—a prerogative of "insiders." If you are fluent in the language and technically competent, you might interpret such a style as terse, compact, and to the point. However, if the person reading or listening to the content is not technically competent or is not fluent in the language, the message can be obscure.

There are a number of grammatical and syntax errors you can avoid that will make your instruction clear and understandable.

The items that follow refer to English. If English is not the language in which you will develop training, consider the difficulties that your target language can present to a non-native speaker and try to avoid those.

Avoid ambiguous modifiers. Modifiers are phrases with two or more adjectives or nouns. Sometimes it is not clear which words are being modified, and which words comprise a phrase. Consider the following instruction, for example:

> **UNCLEAR**　You should understand the process in which the interconnection time error monitor determines accumulated errors.

Does this refer to an error monitor that counts interconnection time, or does it refer to monitoring interconnection time errors?

> **BETTER**　You should understand that interconnection time is monitored, and that the error monitor counts accumulated errors.

Avoid words and phrases with multiple meanings. This includes using words and phrases that can be confusing, or that have culturally inappropriate meanings. Consider the following phrase:

> **UNCLEAR**　Database operating

Out of context, the reader might wonder if the content under this heading provides instructions for operating a database, or if it is a message that informs the reader that a database is now running.

> **BETTER**　How to operate a database
>
> 　　　　　　The database is running.

Avoid ambiguous conjunctions. Conjunctions are words that join sentences, such as *and* and *or*. When several are used in a sentence, what they refer to can be unclear. For example:

UNCLEAR   PCB-contaminated electrical equipment is any electrical equipment that contains 45 ppm or greater PCB but less than 450 ppm and oil-filled electrical equipment other than circuit breakers or reclosers or cables whose PCB concentration is unknown and assumed to be PCB-contaminated electrical equipment.

BETTER   PCB-contaminated electrical equipment is defined as any electrical equipment that contains more than 45 ppm but less than 450 ppm of PCB. This includes, but is not limited to, transformers and circuit breakers. With the exception of circuit breakers, reclosers, and cable, any oil-filled electrical equipment must be treated as PCB-contaminated electrical equipment.

Avoid telegraphic phrases. Telegraphic writing omits articles such as *a, an, the*; conjunctions such as *as* and *or*; and pronouns such as *that*. For example:

UNCLEAR   PCB is toxic when ingested, absorbed by skin, inhaled, considered persistent contaminant, not biodegradable.

BETTER   PCB is toxic when it is ingested, absorbed by the skin, or inhaled. It is considered a persistent environmental contaminant that is not biodegradable.

Avoid grammar that makes plural and singular amounts unclear. For example:

UNCLEAR   Change the modem and server settings.

How many setting changes are there, and for how many of each type of equipment? Is there a setting change for one modem and one server, more than one setting change for multiple modems and servers, or a combination of these options?

BETTER   • Change the settings for the modem and server.

- Change the settings for all modems and servers.

- Change the following two settings on each modem, and one setting on each server.

Avoid dangling modifiers. Modifiers are phrases that are supposed to emphasize a word or phrase. Modifiers that are not clearly associated with what they modify are called dangling modifiers. For example:

UNCLEAR   Also provided on CD, students can complete knowledge tests on basic products and their features.

What is provided on the CD? It immediately modifies students, which does not make sense, and leaves the reader to wonder whether it is supposed to modify tests, products, or features.

BETTER   Students can complete knowledge tests, which are available on CD, on topics such as products and their features.

Avoid long sentences. In a learning environment, shorter sentences help to clarify points. Use two or three sentences instead of one long one.

UNCLEAR   Computer-based testing allows you to skip questions, mark them, or return to them later, so that during the examination you may change your answers as you watch the clock on the screen, which indicates the time remaining so that before exiting the examination you can check for the questions you were unsure of or did not mark.

BETTER   Computer-based testing allows you to skip questions, mark them, and return to them later. You may change your answers. The test is timed, so watch the clock on the screen. It indicates the time remaining before you must exit the test. Before you exit, check the test for questions that you were unsure of or did not mark.

Use punctuation to facilitate understanding. Punctuation gives clues about how words, phrases, and ideas link together. For example:

UNCLEAR	The Computer Emergency Response Team (CERT) is chartered to work with the Internet community to facilitate its response to computer security events involving Internet hosts to take proactive steps to raise the community's awareness of computer security issues and to conduct research that improves the security of existing systems whose products and services include 24-hour technical assistance for responding to computer security incidents, product vulnerability assistance, technical documents and tutorials.
BETTER	The charter of the Computer Emergency Response Team (CERT) is to work with the Internet community to make CERT more responsive to computer security events that involve Internet hosts. CERT takes proactive steps to raise the Internet community's awareness of computer security issues, and to conduct research that improves the security of existing systems. Products and services offered by CERT include: 24-hour technical assistance during computer security incidents, assistance in determining product vulnerability, and support in the form of technical documents and tutorials.

Avoid symbols, abbreviations, and non-standard industry acronyms. Symbols that seem common to you might not commonly be used in the context that you mean, even in countries that speak the same language.

For example, while teaching in England, Scotland, Wales, and Canada, I found that I could not use the symbol # because my students did not recognize it as representing *number*, as in #4 for Number 4. The common abbreviation for *number* was *No.* The abbreviation *i.e.* was not commonly used for *that is*, and *e.g.* was not commonly used in place of *for example*. Those terms were written out, not abbreviated.

The common convention for introducing acronyms is to write out the word or phrase it represents, followed by the acronym, enclosed in parentheses. After its introduction in that manner, the acronym can be used. An exception is where the acronym has two meanings in the same document or lesson. For example, PCB is used in the same industry to represent power circuit breaker and polychlorinated biphenyl.

Define jargon and test its appropriateness. Jargon is specialized language that sounds nonsensical to people outside of the circle in which it is used. In specialized industries, jargon is not only common, but also necessary for creating communication that has specific meaning. It is appropriate for that industry.

Jargon is acceptable in a training course, but there are guidelines for using it.

- **Define each term** the first time it is presented. The term *channel*, for example, has many meanings. Five different meanings in three example industries include: three definitions in the context of internetworking, one definition in the context of marketing, and another definition in television broadcasting.

- **Add a glossary** to the end of your student guide or instructor guide if your course has many jargon terms. If your course includes an electronic format, think about inserting a glossary as a file or option.

- **Test the accuracy and appropriateness** of jargon by including members from the target population in the course development or content review. If you do not, then you risk embarrassment, confusion, or unintended laughter.

- For example, *on the job (OTJ)* is a commonly used term in the United States that refers to training or activities done at work during the course of a workday. When I used the acronym OTJ with a power company customer, he became confused about my meaning. In his industry, on the job was a common term, but OTJ was not—it had an industry-specific meaning. When I used *on the job* in England, I was met with laughter. I discovered that in the U.K., on the job has a nonwork-related meaning, which is sexual in nature. The term was not appropriately used in business.

Conventions of Measure, Counting, and Time

Include units of measure, methods of counting, and notations of time that are familiar to each target audience. Include the alternative in parentheses, for example: They traveled 50 miles (80 km).

International units that differ from the United States include:

Distance. One mile equals 1.6 kilometers, one foot equals 0.3 meters, and one inch equals 2.54 centimeters.

Speed. Fifty miles per hour equals 80 kilometers per hour. Convert miles per hour (mph) into kilometers per hour (kph) by multiplying mph by 8/5. Convert kph to mph by multiplying kph by 5/8.

Weight. One pound equals 0.45 kilograms. One stone equals 6.3 kilograms or 14 pounds.

Temperature. Thirty-two degrees Fahrenheit equals zero degrees Celsius (32° F = 0° C). Degrees Celsius equals degrees Fahrenheit minus 32, times 5/9. Degrees Fahrenheit equals 9/5 times degrees Celsius, plus 32. These conversions are expressed algebraically as follows:

$$C = (F - 32) \times \tfrac{5}{9}$$

$$F = (\tfrac{9}{5} \times C) + 32$$

Time. Many countries express time using 24-hour notation. For courses that will be taught in the United States as well as other countries, include 24-hour notation after times using *a.m.* and *p.m.* For example: Class will begin at 8:00 a.m. (0800) and end at 5:00 p.m. (1700). Do not use punctuation or the word *hours* with 24-hour notation.

INCORRECT   at 1700 hours

CORRECT   at 1700

Date. Internationally, dates might be expressed with the day preceding the month, that is, date/month/year. In this case, providing a date in numbers in one convention, then in parentheses in another convention, as you did with units of measure, distance, and time, serves to confuse rather than clarify. To avoid confusion, write the name of the month: 10 January 2001, or January 10, 2001. You can also provide a key, such as dd/mm/yyyy, to indicate the convention you are using.

Exponential notation. An exponential number might need to be expressed in a different way from what you are used to. For example, I learned to express 4 x 4 x 4 exponentially as 4^3. An internetworking customer, for whom English was a second language, asked me to express exponents for multilingual people like himself, in the following manner: N-to-the-power-of-x, which for our example would be *four-to-the-power-of-three*. He said that verbally expressing the notation as *four cubed* or *four to the third power*, or writing the expression with a superscript or without hyphens between the words, was confusing.

Frames of Reference

A frame of reference is a point of view that indicates some form of bias. It can be geographic, national, racial, religious, cultural, or any number of other points of view. If you are unaware of your frames of reference, then your course content can inadvertently exclude or alienate groups of the target audience. References that you should monitor include:

Seasons. References to seasons have a six-month difference in meaning to residents of the Southern Hemisphere. If your intended meaning is a specific month of the year, name the month. If it is a period of the year, name the fiscal quarter.

UNCLEAR   New products are announced during the winter months.

BETTER   New products are announced during the fourth quarter of each year.

New products are announced from December through February.

Centric phrases. Terms that assume that the listener or reader has a specific point of view are called centric. For example, a nation-centric phrase is *domestic*. Domestic trading partner assumes that the trading partner is in the same nation as the speaker. If your course is written in the United States and refers to a domestic trading partner, meaning a trading partner that is in the United States, what you mean can be confusing to an audience in Austria. Centric terms require the reader to translate not only your words, but also your intent.

Phrases that exclude others are centric, for example, *non-US*. Instead, use *within the United States* and *outside of the United States*.

Names of organizations. Avoid assumptions about frames of reference by referring to organizations by their complete names. For example,

UNCLEAR   The federal government, the state government, the city government, the military

BETTER   The Canadian government, the Fujian Province government, the City of Mannheim government, the U.S. Army

Numerical amounts. The numerical term *trillion* seems unique to North America. I have been corrected by South American and European customers, who have told me that they verbally express the number one followed by nine zeros (one trillion in the U.S.) as 1,000 million. Sometimes the British use *milliard*, which is a word that derives from Old French and means million.

Gestures

Prepare instructors for international training delivery by finding out what gestures have special meanings. *Come here* gestures are different among countries, and in Asian countries you can insult someone by doing it the wrong way.

Methods of counting. Instructors should not depend on communicating a message by counting with their hands. Numbers are represented with different fingers in different countries. For example, the Chinese gesture for the number ten is to cross the middle fingers to form an X. North Americans could easily misinterpret this gesture as a double insult. In Asian countries, ten might also be expressed by tapping both fists together, or touching the fingertips of both hands with the palms facing down. Some countries count starting with the little finger, others with the thumb.

Add Value by Learning International Needs

Claims about understanding worldwide customers are hard to believe when the language or gestures used to express those ideas exclude the target audience. Make the effort to understand the needs of your international audience. Include them in the design and development process.

Repurposing
Documentation to Training

Repurpose means using existing material in a context or for a purpose other than what it was developed for. This can mean taking documentation, help, or other non-training material and transforming it to meet a training purpose. The chapter on customizing described how to use existing training material. This chapter focuses on how to select and adapt material not intended for training and convert it to useable training content.

The table below is from the chapter on assessing training development skills. It compares information design with instructional design. These differences can serve as a guide for you in this chapter as you think about selecting, adapting, and using existing material for training.

Documentation	Training
• Is an information product	• Enables through experiences
• Increases understanding	• Develops skills and knowledge
• Focuses on a task: how to get from A to Z	• Focuses on job performance: learning what to do and how to do it
• Is organized for information retrieval	
• Scope: one task broken into steps	• Is organized for behavior change
• Customers are called users	• Scope: collection of skills and knowledge required to perform a job
	• Customers are called learners

Table 19-1. Differences between Documentation and Training Products

Review of Differences between Documentation and Training

Information vehicles, such as documentation, help, policies, and procedures, involve how to use features, interpret data, or follow a process. Such information is organized to be visually inviting, easy to access, and intuitive to navigate.

Users usually rely on documentation to answer questions, direct them through a process, or increase their understanding. The scope of information design includes one topic, divided into discrete components. The focus of the approach is how to get from A to Z. It tells the user what to do—*fit the small end of Part One into the hole in Part Two and twist Part One 90 degrees counterclockwise.*

Unlike training, documentation is not designed to answer atypical questions, offer alternative ways to understand a problem, or enable the user to apply the information in another context. Information is designed to inform.

Sometimes documentation does not explain why the task is needed. It does not answer individual questions about what problems the topic will solve, does not share user experiences about similar problems that arise on the job, and typically does not enable users to compare strategies and applications. Instruction does all of these things.

Instruction infuses life into information. It works with learners rather than users. A learner's relationship with course content is dynamic. Instruction enables learners by strategically developing knowledge and skills.

The vehicle for instruction is structured learning experiences; that is, tasks and activities that involve the learner, answer questions, provide a venue for sharing experiences, and that apply content to job-related situations.

Sound instruction converts information into something dynamic because learners ask questions like:

- So what?
- What does this mean?
- How can I use it?
- What about doing it another way?
- What options do I have?
- What are others like me doing with this information?

Preliminary Documentation Selection

You can target existing material for repurposing once you have developed a project plan, but you cannot determine what changes the material requires or which specific tasks it will be used to perform until you have a design document.

Not all documentation about a topic is appropriate content for instruction. How do you select what is appropriate?

Objectives drive content selection. If you have read the eight chapters about a systematic approach to training development, you might remember that the course goal and objectives drive your selection of course content.

Content selection criteria. Your primary selection criteria for existing documentation are that you can use it with minimal adaptation, and that it supports the course objectives and design. Material that does not have a matching focus or that is not easily adaptable should be set aside.

Organizing for Easy Recall

You might use many resources, or many selections from a large resource. When you are ready to repurpose the content, how can you ensure that you can find the selections that you reviewed?

Document your resources. Use a tool like the Matrix for Organizing Documentation Resources to link the learning objective, topic, and resource.

Note information gaps. Note questions that need to be answered, and topics that have no material.

Rate your resources, so that if you run short of time, you can prioritize your efforts.

Example

The following example illustrates how to organize documents and other resources for easy recall during the content development step.

The target population in this example is emergency medical response services (EMS) professionals.

The course goal is to enable professional rescuers—those with a duty to respond to a life-threatening situation—with the skills needed to react appropriately to respiratory and cardiac emergencies.

The course objectives are to enable EMS professionals to:

1. Describe their role as professional rescuers within the emergency medical services (EMS) system.

2. Recognize and appropriately respond to respiratory and cardiac emergencies in infants, children, and adults.

3. Perform cardio-pulmonary resuscitation (CPR).

Course Objective	Topics	Questions, Resources, Ratings
1. Describe their role as professional rescuers within the emergency medical services (EMS) system.	• Certification levels and agencies	• What are specialized requirements for EMS professionals, and who are the certifying agencies? Resource: Red Cross CPR program (good), EMS Emergency Network Handbook, Pages 110-189 (excellent). City and State legal guidelines (quality varies with state). • What care do professional rescuers provide? • What care might the victim be getting when EMT arrives at the scene, and by whom? • Need: Statistics about pre-EMT arrival care of victims

Table 19-2. Matrix for Organizing Documentation Resources

Course Objective	Topics	Questions, Resources, Ratings
2. Recognize and appropriately respond to, respiratory and cardiac emergencies in infants, children, and adults.	• Factors that cause respiratory distress and trauma • Symptoms of emergency distress and trauma • Differences in response to victims based on age and health condition	• What factors cause respiratory distress and trauma? • What symptoms constitute an emergency for infants, children, and adults? • Are there additional considerations for advanced-aged adults? • What are appropriate responses for each type of victim?
3. Perform specialized skills and techniques used by professional rescuers.	• Certification renewal • How to perform CPR • CPR gear	• What are the consequences of not meeting and maintaining certification requirements? • What are the specialized skills and techniques that EMS professionals need to know? • What gear is required for learning CPR, for conducting CPR on real-life victims?

Table 19-2, continued. Matrix for Organizing Documentation Resources

How to Repurpose Documentation

Once you have sorted the selected documentation by objective, you are ready to look more closely at the content and make decisions about what fits exactly, and what requires adaptation. Do this after completing the design document.

Use a matrix like the Checklist for Assessing Content for Repurposing to help you evaluate a resource and fit it into specific training tasks.

Learning Objective: Describe the emergency care that professional rescuers provide.

Topic: Factors that help or complicate care that rescuers provide

Resource: Police reports from 400 rescue missions in five eastern states

Content Description:	Example Comments
Does this content apply to more than one learning objective? If so, select one to which it will apply.	The content best fits this objective.
If the content is not an exact fit, what must be done to make it fit, in terms of focus and function?	Extract information about who was caring for the patient when the EMS team arrived, whether they were currently certified in CPR or first aid, and whether CPR was being administered.
How much adaptation of this resource is required in terms of time, money, and effort?	Extracting enough information to create statistics will take about 50 hours. The statistics would be nice to have, and add credibility. Not worth the effort. Extracting representative examples will take about 10 hours. Examples are important for this topic. Worth the effort.
How can the content best be used? (As an example, in an activity, exercise, or test question)	To add impact to content, as test questions, as examples for role play situations.
What jargon, acronyms, and job-specific phrases need to be deleted or added to make this material specific to the learners?	It is appropriate as is.

Table 19-3. Checklist for Assessing Content for Repurposing

Ready-to-Use Scripts

There are many instructional tasks that you can electronically automate by inserting programming scripts into server applications, or by embedding them into browser-based instructional material.

Appropriate tasks for automation include course activities that test, assess, survey, drill, reinforce, and require choices.

The purpose of this chapter is to introduce you to ready-to-use scripts, guidelines for using them, programming languages that they are readily available in, and web sites with scripts that can be adapted for e-learning courses.

Guidelines

Ready-to-use scripts add dynamic function and interactivity without spending a lot of money or development time.

If your instructional design calls for a pre-course test, end-of-course test, post-course test, survey, questionnaire, or assessment, then automating this function could save paperwork and the personnel requirements of administering, collecting, and tabulating results. Ready-to-use scripts are also appropriate solutions where learner access needs to be available worldwide, or 24 hours a day, seven days a week.

Learning objectives drive the training design. Instructional activities support the design.

Ready-to-use scripts can also save administrative time by automating registration, learner confirmation, billing, and other pre-course functions.

Ready-to-use scripts are not appropriate to use if solely for the purpose of adding a computer-based component to your course. An easy to complete paper-based quiz that has an overlay grading key, or that can be graded by learners in class, could have a higher learning value than a computer-based component, and for a lower investment of time, money, and effort. Let your choices be guided by the following mantra:

Learning objectives drive the training design.

Instructional activities support the design.

What Is Available

You might have the programming skills to develop scripts yourself. This task requires that you be able to program, install, debug, and customize the script. You might have the skills, but do you have the time to do it? Consider what is ready-to-use and whether you can adapt it to suit the needs of your course.

You can download workable, customizable scripts free from the Internet. Testing scripts include multiple choice, matching, and fill-in-the blank test items. You can download tests in game format that are patterned after *Jeopardy*, *Hangman*, and crossword puzzles. You can download them from the Tech Writer's Guide site (http://www.lepublishing.com) or find them at sites listed in the resource appendix. All you need to do is customize them by inserting words and phrases that pertain to your course topics. Even *Who Wants to be a Millionaire?* can be purchased for $39 US. http://www.cgi.notts.net/rs/gmathews/quiz.html

Form creation is available on some web page software, as well as at sites with downloadable, ready-to-use scripts. These scripts are often imbedded into HTML or linked to a database management program such as FoxBase, Access, or DataBasePro.

An overview of major authoring tools and programming languages used to build web sites are described at the Web Developer's Virtual Library. http://www.stars.com/Authoring

Common Script Programming Languages

Common Gateway Interface (CGI) scripts are small programs that reside in the server. They enable the user to receive dynamic information on a web page in response to variables the user submits, such as test results, after submitting a completed test.

CGI scripts enable web sites to interact with databases and other applications. For example, I have created pools of test questions in Microsoft Word that were imported into DataBasePro and combined with CGI scripts to create intranet tests that randomly selected questions, returned feedback, and generated test results.

Java, modeled after C++, is an interpreted programming language. It cannot run by itself. It requires an interpreter, which translates and runs the Java program at the same time.

This is an asset, because it means that Java can run on any hardware that runs a Java interpreter—it is cross-platform. You need to write only one version of it to work on all of your sites.

Java supports networks, such as the Internet and intranets. It can be used to develop stand-alone applications, as well as applications embedded into web pages.

A Java program called from the client machine by a web page is called a Java applet. When the program runs on a server it is called a servlet. A stand-alone Java program is called a Java application.

228 Developing Training Courses ▶ **Manage and Customize**

JavaScript is basically a macro language for HTML page development. It is a different language from Java. It uses syntax similar to Java, but it is not compiled into bytecode. It remains in source code embedded within an HTML document and is translated one line at time into machine code by the JavaScript-enabled browser. It can access data from other components on the page. It can be used, for example, for form validation.

Practical Extraction Report Language (Perl) is a programming language that uses UNIX syntax. It is designed to handle system administrator and string-handling functions. It has been adapted to non-UNIX platforms, and is used widely to write web server programs

Typical programs in Perl are authored for tasks such as automatically updating user accounts and newsgroup postings, processing removal requests, synchronizing databases, and generating reports.

Where to Find Scripts

Programming scripts designed to facilitate computer-based training development, including both testing and interactive features, are often free and downloadable from the Internet from a number of sites. My purpose here, however, is not to review them, nor is the list complete. I have only named the products that I am aware of to help you find your way.

A few examples of where to find scripts that include tests, quizzes, games, and interactive exercises are listed below. A more extensive list that includes course administration resources is in the appendix.

- Cut and Paste JavaScript web site.
  http://www.infohiway.com/javascript/indexf.htm

- Freebie.com lists free CGI and Java scripts.
  http://www.freebielist.com/scripts.htm

- Free Code has a small selection of tests and surveys. What makes this site worth visiting is the variety of code available

that can support your online course.
http://www.freecode.com/onlineapp.html

- JavaScript World lists many scripts that can be adapted for interactive exercises in training programs.
  http://www.jsworld.com

- Matt's Script Archive contains CGI scripts that can add interest to your online course.
  http://www.worldwidemart.com/scripts

- Free Perl CGI downloads from Matt's Script Archive, such as:

  - *Random Text* can be used to highlight or reinforce online course content.
    http://www.worldwidemart.com/scripts/rand_text.shtml

  - *Countdown* can be used to assist learners who are working on timed activities online, such as tests or skill practice.
    http://www.worldwidemart.com/scripts/countdown.shtml

- Perl Archive. Perl scripts for applications, web pages, and servers:
  http://www.Perlarchive.com/guide/Tests_and_Quizzes

- Script Search web site, which includes:

  - Interactive surveys and voting:
    http://scriptsearch.internet.com/pages/l18c7c39.shtml

  - Interactive Java tests and quizzes:
    http://scriptsearch.internet.com/pages/l18c7c41.shtml

  - Interactive JavaScript tests and quizzes:
    http://scriptsearch.internet.com/pages/l4c7c41.shtml

  - Interactive Perl tests and quizzes:
    http://scriptsearch.internet.com/pages/l9c7c41.shtml

- Tech Writer's Guide is my site. It provides customizable templates for training developers, how-to articles, and downloadable files that can make your course development task easier. http://www.lepublishing.com

- Web Developer's Virtual Library provides excellent, links and sources for web site developers that range from beginner to advanced levels. Good source for online course administration tools. http://wdvl.internet.com

Section 4:
Appendices

Job Aids

The job aid appendix is a listing of where to find tables in the book that include guidelines, checklists, assessments, and templates that can assist you in your course development tasks.

Bibliography of References

These are the bibliographic listings for sources named in the text as footnotes or references.

"1998 Survey of STC Consultants and Independent Contractors Special Interest Group (CICSIG)." Society for Technical Communication. Online. July 13, 2000. Unavailable.

American Society of Training and Development. *ASTD Trainer's Toolkit: Job Descriptions in Workplace Learning and Performance.* Washington, D.C.: ASTD, n.d.

Bassi, Laurie J. and Mark E. Van Buren. "1998 ASTD State of the Industry Report." *T&D Journal.* January, 1998.

Bloom, Benjamin S. *Taxonomy of Educational Objectives: The Classification of Educational Goals.* London: Longman Group, 1969.

Jacobson, Peggy Ph.D. "So You Think You Want to Be a Technical Writer?" STC Job Fair. Bellevue, WA. 8 Nov. 2000.

Kroeger, Otto and Janet M. Thuesen. *Type Talk: The 16 Personality Types that Determine How We Live, Love, and Work.* New York: Delta, 1988.

Rackham, Neil. *Major Account Sales Strategy.* New York: McGraw-Hill, 1989.

Rothwell, William J. and Henry J. Sredl. *ASTD Reference Guide to Professional Human Resource Development Roles and Competencies.* Volume 1, 2nd ed. Washington, D.C.: ASTD, n.d.

Bibliography
of Resources

Resources are listed below for topics that relate to developing training courses. This is just a starter list. A search through bibliographies in printed material and of keywords for online material will help you to find more.

Instructional Technology

Driscoll, Margaret. *Web-Based Training: Using Technology to Design Adult Learning Experiences*. San Francisco: Jossey-Bass/Pfeiffer, 1998.

Edvinsson, L., M. S. Malone. *Intellectual Capital: Realizing Your Company's True Value by Finding Its Hidden Roots*. New York: HarperBusiness, 1997.

Gagné, R.M. *The Conditions of Learning*. 4th ed. New York: Holt, Rinehart and Winston, 1997.

Harless, Joe H. *An Ounce of Analysis*. Newnan, Georgia: Harless Performance Guild, 1975.

Head, G.E. *Training Cost Analysis: A How-to Guide for Trainers and Managers*. Alexandria, Virginia: American Society for Training and Development, 1993.

Jonassen, D.H., W. H. Hannum, M. Tassmen. *A Handbook of Task Analysis Procedures*. Westport, Connecticut: Praeger, 1998.

Knowles, Malcolm. *The Adult Learner: A Neglected Species*. Houston: Gulf Publishing Co., 1973.

Langenbach, Michael Ph.D. *Curriculum Models in Adult Education*. Malabar, Florida: Robert E. Krieger Publishing Company, 1988.

Mager, Robert F. *Goal Analysis: How to Clarify Your Goals So You Can Actually Achieve Them*. 3rd ed. Atlanta: Center for Effective Performance, 1997.

_____. *Preparing Instructional Objectives: A Critical Tool in the Development of Effective Instruction*. 3rd ed. Atlanta: Center for Effective Performance, 1977.

Rossett, A. *Training Needs Assessment*. Englewood Cliffs, New Jersey: Educational Technology Publications, 1987.

Rossett, A., J. Gauthier-Dawnes. *A Handbook of Job Aids*. San Francisco: Pfeiffer, 1991.

Wilson, B. G., D. H. Jonassen, and P. Cole. "Cognitive Approaches to Instructional Design." G. M. Piskurich, Editor. *The ASTD Handbook of Instructional Technology*. New York: McGraw-Hill, 1993. 21.1-21.22. Online. Internet. December 17, 2000. Available: http://www.cudenver.edu/~bwilson/training.html. Includes article in its entirety and a bibliography.

Performance Technology

Gilbert, Thomas F. *Human Competence—Engineering Worthy Performance*. New York: McGraw Hill, 1978.

Stolovitch, H. D., Erica J. Keeps. *Handbook of Human Performance Technology: Improving Individual and Organizational Performance Worldwide*. San Francisco: Jossey-Bass/Pfeiffer Publishers, 1999.

Technical Communication

Lists of Web Sites for Technical Communicators includes lots of helpful and interesting categories and links, with annotated descriptions of what they contain. http://www.spiritone.com/~petec/Marilynn/website_list.html

TechWr-L is an award-winning web site that includes almost every kind of resource support that a technical writer could wish for, including information about developing web-based training. http://www.raycomm.com/techwhirl/sitemap.html

E-Learning

Blackboard.com is a self-described end-to-end e-learning platform that includes course administration features. http://blackboard.com/

Learning Circuits, a public online magazine published by ASTD that covers e-learning topics. http://www.learningcircuits.com

Training 2000 Buyer's Guide: The Directory of Computer Training and Support Products and Services. Volume 3, Number 11. Inside Technology Training. December, 1999. http://ittrain.com

Web-Based Training Information Center, also includes distance and online learning information. http://www.filename.com/wbt

Training Development

Multimedia Development Tools is a Georgia Tech University web site. It has free checklists and ideas for analysis, design, management, production, and evaluation tasks. The ASTD web site also provided a link to it.
http://mime1.marc.gatech.edu/MM_Tools

Training Basics page at the American Society of Training and Development (ASTD) site, which appear to be of most help if you are in the content development step of development or are delivering training.
http://www.astd.org/virtual_community/comm_trainbasics/tools_links.html

International Markets

A More Perfect Union (AMPU) Guide: Common Cross-cultural Communications Challenges.
http://www.wwcd.org/action/ampu/crosscult.html

The Web of Cultures site provides a list of gestures and their meanings, organized by areas of the world, then by countries.
http://www.webofculture.com/refs/gestures.html

Ready-to-Use Scripts

Activity Maker is software from Gepeto Software ($10). It creates worksheets, puzzles, and quizzes from vocabulary lists that you enter. Just a few clicks, and you have word search puzzles, crossword puzzles, any of five types of quizzes, scramble worksheets, secret code activities, and more. There's a wide variety of extra features, including the ability to import word lists from Vocab-Flash, and the ability to export worksheets to word processors for the addition of clip art. It has an option for foreign language symbols and letters. Version 2.0 features new worksheet editing tools to add clip art and the ability to change colors, fonts, and sizes. Order it from CNET download.com.
http://download.cnet.com/downloads/0-1635591-100-1772898.html?tag=st.dl.1635591-106-1.lst-1-4.1772898

Cut-N-Paste Java Script Home has a free crossword puzzle at this URL. http://www.infohiway.com/javascript/cross/index.htm

Extropia products in PERL include MC quiz grader, and benchmark with other learners. http://www.extropia.com/products.html

Quick Quiz, for UNIX and Windows NT users is a free Perl script that runs on UNIX or Windows NT that can be used as a Quiz or Survey Tool. As a survey tool, you can run a multiple-choice questionnaire and collect all the data in a tab-delimited ASCII file. As a quiz tool you can return the score, show the average, the percentile, the grade, display the answers, e-mail the results and track the top scorers. http://www.bytesinteractive.com/qq.htm

The PERL Archive: Tests and Quizzes. http://www.perlarchive.com/guide/Tests_and_Quizzes/ ,http://www.perlarchive.com/guide/Tests_and_Quizzes/next2.s html

Who Wants to Be A Millionaire? This is a multiple-choice CGI game script that you can purchase and download for $39 US. http://www.cgi.notts.net/rs/gmathews/quiz.html

Knowledge Management

Davenport, Thomas and Laurence Prusak. *Working Knowledge: How Organizations Manage What They Know.* Boston: Harvard Business School Press, 1999.

Knowledge Management Portal, managed by Brint.com, has links galore on this hot topic. http://www.brint.com/km/

Multimedia

The Directory of Video, Computer, & Audio-visual Products. 42nd ed. Fairfax, Virginia: International Communications Industries Association, 1997-98. $120. The 42nd edition for 1997-98 includes audio/visual production and projection equipment, furniture, and accessories.

Multimedia & Videodisk Compendium for Education & Training.
10th ed. St. Paul. Minnesota: Emerging Technology
Consultants, Inc., 1998. $45. This resource covers almost 4,600
videodisk and CD-ROM titles. It includes short product
descriptions, price, hardware compatibility, audience or grade
level, and vendor contact information. It covers subjects such
as business, electronic technology, industrial safety, computer
training, and health care. It also includes a directory of
authoring systems, authoring tools, and multimedia
presentation systems, including an index to titles and a list of
professional organizations and publications that serve the laser
disk industry.

The National Information Center for Educational Media (NICEM)
database, includes 630,000 educational audiovisual products. It
is targeted primarily for educational institutions. The database
can be searched by subject, age level, and media type. It
includes instructional media producers and distributors, along
with their addresses and phone numbers. Access to the
database starts at $500 per year. http://www.nicem.com

The Training Media Review (TMR) web site provides reviews of
media-based business training products, and offers training
consulting services. The site also includes media review
communities comprised of peers, and organized by key
business training topics. http://www.tmreview.com

Video Quest, Inc. of Cleveland, Ohio, offers more than 1,000
training videos for rent or purchase in their online catalog.
Multimedia clips are available for some videos, which can be
ordered online. http://www.vidquest.com/catalog.html

Glossary

24 x 7, or 24/7. Available 24 hours per day, seven days per week.

assessment. A tool that helps appraise, evaluate, rank, or estimate.

CD. Compact disk.

chapter. An instructional unit within a course.

content analysis. A part of the analysis step in course development in which you collect information about the tasks and documentation related to a job. Also *task analysis*, which is the form preferred in this guide.

context analysis. A part of the analysis step in course development in which you collect information about the environment in which the training will occur, or in which it will be developed. Also *training environment analysis*, which is the form preferred in this guide.

course. A collection of instructional topics and activities, related by a single course goal.

curriculum. A group of related courses, for example, a network-engineering curriculum.

deliverables. Items that are in finished form, and are usually tangible, such as instructor guides, learner guides, PowerPoint presentations, handouts, tests, web sites, and compact disks.

e-learning. One of the many terms used to describe learning that uses a computer as instructional media.

facilitator. An instructional style that uses minimal lecture, and facilitates student interaction and discovery of the learning points.

instructional media. The equipment and tools that are used in a learning environment, such as transparency film, PowerPoint slide presentations, projectors, instructional web pages, and videotapes.

instructional methods. Procedures that the training developer determines will create an effective learning environment, such as lecture, case study, and testing.

instructional systems design. A systematic plan for creating learning environments.

instructional technology. The application of studies about adult learning to corporate settings.

instructor. The term usually used in a corporate setting for a corporate teacher. Also trainer.

just in time (JIT). The practice of delivering training as it is needed, rather than anticipating need and training in advance of it. The concept is that this practice saves money, trains only the people who will use the training, provides chunks of training rather than a whole course, and delivers training immediately prior to implementation of what will be learned, thus not allowing the learner a chance to forget it.

learner analysis. A part of the analysis step in course development in which you determine the skills and knowledge gap between the training population and those who are proficient in the targeted tasks.

modular training. A training course delivered in units that may be taken out of order without affecting the impact of the learning.

module. A collection of related chapters within a course.

performance technology. The application of studies about job performance to corporate settings.

pilot. The first delivery of a training course. Sometimes called beta.

ROI. Return on investment, which is difficult to determine about training programs unless you have determined and agreed upon measurement parameters prior to training development.

script. A file in programming code that performs some function, and that can be inserted into an HTML document or other type of electronic file.

SME. Subject matter expert. Sometimes called an SE, but this is confusing in a computer technology field that has systems engineers, also called SEs.

stakeholder. A person who has a decision-making power or accountability in a task or project.

structured learning experience. 1. A training design. 2. An exercise or activity that leads a learner to discover a learning point through personal experience.

T&D. Training and development.

task analysis. A part of the analysis step in course development in which you collect information about the training environment. Also *content analysis.*

trainer. A term used in a corporate setting for a teacher. Also instructor.

training development. The design and development of instructional systems and programs. Also *instructional design and development.*

training environment analysis. A part of the analysis step in course development in which you collect information about the environment in which the training will occur, or in which it will be developed. Also *context analysis.*

verifiable verb. A verb that indicates observable, measurable behavior, such as *count* or *describe*. A criterion of a measurable objective.

Index

Learning Edge Publishing

Visit *Tech Writer's Guide* at the Learning Edge Publishing web site (www.lepublishing.com)—where technical writers go for training development answers.

Use the handy order form on the next page to order additional books.

Service Guarantee

If you are not satisfied with any product you order, return it for a full refund.

Your personal information will not be sold or shared with any other company or organization.

Quick Order Form

Fax: Dial (253) 588-1594 and send this form.

Telephone: Call (253) 588-5174, and have your credit card ready.

E-mail: service@lepublishing.com, and include the contact information on this form. This method is *not secure*, so please do not include your credit card information. We will phone you.

Post: Please send your order form and payment (make check or money order payable in U.S. currency) to Learning Edge Publishing, PO Box 97041, Tacoma, Washington 98497-0041.

Add $5.00 for shipping, and, for State of Washington addresses, also add $2.55 (8.5% tax).

Please check if you would like information about:

- ☐ Other publications
- ☐ Seminars, speaking engagements
- ☐ Mailing lists
- ☐ Consulting services
- ☐ Quantity or customized orders

Name:_____

Address:_____

_____

City:_____

State/Province:_____ Zip/Postal Code:_____

Country:_____

Phone:_____

E-mail:_____

___Visa   ___MasterCard   Expires (mm/yy) _____

Card Number:_____

Name on card:_____

Signature:_____

Learning Edge Publishing

Visit *Tech Writer's Guide* at the Learning Edge Publishing web site (www.lepublishing.com)—where technical writers go for training development answers.

Use the handy order form on the next page to order additional books.

Service Guarantee

If you are not satisfied with any product you order, return it for a full refund.

Your personal information will not be sold or shared with any other company or organization.

Quick Order Form

Fax: Dial (253) 588-1594 and send this form.

Telephone: Call (253) 588-5174, and have your credit card ready.

E-mail: service@lepublishing.com, and include the contact information on this form. This method is *not secure*, so please do not include your credit card information. We will phone you.

Post: Please send your order form and payment (make check or money order payable in U.S. currency) to Learning Edge Publishing, PO Box 97041, Tacoma, Washington 98497-0041.

Add $5.00 for shipping, and, for State of Washington addresses, also add $2.55 (8.5% tax).

Please check if you would like information about:

- ☐ Other publications
- ☐ Seminars, speaking engagements
- ☐ Mailing lists
- ☐ Consulting services
- ☐ Quantity or customized orders

Name:_____

Address:_____

_____

City:_____

State/Province:_____ Zip/Postal Code:_____

Country:_____

Phone:_____

E-mail:_____

___Visa ___MasterCard   Expires (mm/yy) _____

Card Number:_____

Name on card:_____

Signature:_____